Android Apps

FOR

DUMMIES®

Amazing
Android™ Apps
FOR
DUMMIES®

by Daniel A. Begun

WILEY

Wiley Publishing, Inc.

Amazing Android™ Apps For Dummies®

Published by
Wiley Publishing, Inc.
111 River Street
Hoboken, NJ 07030-5774
www.wiley.com

For general information on our other products and services, please contact our Customer Care Department within the U.S. at 877-762-2974, outside the U.S. at 317-572-3993, or fax 317-572-4002.

For technical support, please visit www.wiley.com/techsupport.

Wiley also publishes its books in a variety of electronic formats. Some content that appears in print may not be available in electronic books.

Library of Congress Control Number: 2010943064

ISBN: 978-0-470-93629-0

Manufactured in the United States of America

10 9 8 7 6 5 4 3 2 1

WILEY

About the Author

Daniel A. Begun still doesn't know what he wants to be when he grows up. But until he figures it out, he'll continue to have fun as a technology journalist, where he gets to play with lots of cool gadgets and apps.

In his 20 years of working in technology journalism, Daniel has written for numerous top technology publications and Web sites, including CNET, Computerworld, *Computer Shopper*, ExtremeTech, HotHardware.com, *Laptop* magazine, Maximum PC, and *PC Magazine*. Daniel is the former Labs Director for CNET, where he ran CNET's product testing labs for many years.

Dedication

This book is dedicated to my amazing, supportive, understanding, patient wife, Caren; and to my beautiful, brilliant, funny, fiercely independent daughter, Sarah.

Author's Acknowledgments

A huge thanks goes out to Bill Dyszel, author of *Outlook 2010 For Dummies,* who first brought me into the Wiley fold. I also must profess a profuse thank-you to Katie Mohr at Wiley for being a tireless advocate for this project, as well as for being extraordinarily understanding when life had a habit of interfering with my deadlines.

A monumental thank-you to the entire editorial team at Wiley who helped whip this book into shape. Special thanks go to Christopher Morris for his attention to detail, Debbye Butler for her keen eye, and everybody else at Wiley who had a hand in making this book happen.

I also must thank Ashley Lane at the MWW Group for setting me up with a Samsung Epic 4G loaner — which because of its gorgeous-looking screen, turned out to be the Android device I used the most often for evaluating apps and taking screenshots. Thanks also go out to Brian Bennett at Waggener Edstrom Worldwide, who loaned me the speedy HTC Incredible and rugged HTC Legend Android phones. A double thank-you goes to Len Fernandes at SierraTech Public Relations and Max Seybold at CherryPal, for letting me get a taste of Android running on a tablet with the 7-inch CherryPad America (C515).

I'd be remiss if I didn't also thank Angela Schapiro and Marjorie Normand for their sage advice and counsel.

Last, but not least, thank you, reader, for buying this book. I hope you find it useful.

Publisher's Acknowledgments

We're proud of this book; please send us your comments at http://dummies.custhelp.com. For other comments, please contact our Customer Care Department within the U.S. at 877-762-2974, outside the U.S. at 317-572-3993, or fax 317-572-4002.

Some of the people who helped bring this book to market include the following:

Acquisitions, Editorial

Sr. Project Editor: Christopher Morris

Acquisitions Editor: Katie Mohr

Copy Editor: Debbye Butler

Editorial Manager: Kevin Kirschner

Editorial Assistant: Amanda Graham

Sr. Editorial Assistant: Cherie Case

Composition Services

Project Coordinator: Sheree Montgomery

Layout and Graphics: Claudia Bell, Carl Byers, Carrie A. Cesavice, Joyce Haughey, Andrea Hornberger

Proofreaders: John Greenough, Mildred Rosenzweig

Publishing and Editorial for Technology Dummies

    Richard Swadley, Vice President and Executive Group Publisher

    Andy Cummings, Vice President and Publisher

    Mary Bednarek, Executive Acquisitions Director

    Mary C. Corder, Editorial Director

Publishing for Consumer Dummies

    Diane Graves Steele, Vice President and Publisher

Composition Services

    Debbie Stailey, Director of Composition Services

Contents at a Glance

Table of Contents

Introduction

Welcome to the very first *Amazing Android Apps For Dummies* book!
I'd like to say this book has been a long time coming, but the truth of
the matter is that Android apps have been around for only a couple of
years, and they're only just now reaching the quality and quantity to
justify such a book. If I had written this book even just a few months
earlier, it would either have been a much thinner book, or I would
have had to call it *Some Amazing but Mostly Mediocre Android Apps For
Dummies*. That's too long a title, and it probably wouldn't make for a
very interesting read.

By some accounts there were more than 150,000 apps available for
Android devices by the end of 2010. That's a lot of apps, and the
number of new apps that come available for Android devices keeps
growing — by the end of 2010, roughly 1,000 new Android apps were
showing up *every* day.

Some of the apps come from large companies that employ a phalanx of
developers. Other apps are created by hobbyists and enthusiasts who
are just getting their programming feet wet. But as I worked on this
book and had occasion to reach out to the developer community time
and time again, I discovered that many Android apps are produced
by knowledgeable programmers, working in their spare time — mostly
because they have a passion for the Android platform. For many
developers, the potential money to be made from producing Android
apps is a secondary concern, if at all.

There are actually far more free Android apps available than paid
apps. And don't assume just because an app is free that it isn't any
good. There are scads of *amazing* free Android apps to be found. And
don't assume, either, that if you find a paid app that meets your needs
or tickles your fancy that there must also be a free app that does the
same thing and is just as good. That might be true in some cases, but
many paid apps are well worth their price tags.

About This Book

Which brings me to the purpose of this book: to try to make some
sense of all these Android apps! It's not humanly possible to sys-
tematically evaluate every single available Android app and decide
if it's worthy of being installed on your device. I know this because I
tried! The apps were coming out faster than I could install them, and
I could only store so many apps on my Android devices before their

storage filled up. I can't keep track of the number of times my devices informed me that their storage were almost full and that I needed to remove some installed apps in order to make room for new apps.

So, yes, I looked at a lot of apps, but I didn't look at all 150,000+ of them. I probably evaluated somewhere in the neighborhood of 700 apps, which were on my radar because they had high Android Market ratings, positive user comments, they were recommended by friends and associates, I saw positive reviews on Web sites, or because I was already using them. (If you don't know what the Android Market is, take a look at my explanation of it in Chapter 1.) I didn't rely purely on this buzz to find worthy apps; I also scoured the Android Market on an almost daily basis looking at new arrivals as well.

I whittled the list down to 190 apps, with 10 apps in each category (chapter). For the most part, the apps fit well into their designated chapters, but several apps could easily fit into multiple chapters. For instance, should the Dolphin Browser HD (a Web browser app) go into the Communications, Productivity, Tools, or Utilities chapter?

I also need to mention that a few of the paid apps I evaluated were provided to me at no cost by their respective developers. But this was only *after* I had already identified the app as a strong candidate for the book — and some of these apps didn't make the cut.

There's also a whole other type of Android app called a widget, which is typically a window that sits on the Android home page that displays information. Many apps include widgets that provide a small subset of their features and act as shortcuts to launching the apps. There simply isn't room in this book to discuss widgets, so I focus purely on apps and their functionality as apps — even if they also include widgets. Perhaps my next project will be *Amazing Android Widgets For Dummies.*

Conventions Used in This Book

Throughout most of the book I use the term *Android device.* The vast majority of Android devices out there are mobile phones, but not all of them are. Another category of Android devices, the Android tablet, is quickly becoming very popular. There are even some portable media players and e-book readers that run the Android operating system. Android devices come in all shapes and sizes, and many of them are capable of running additional apps other than just the ones that they come with. So when you see the words *Android device* in this book, know that I'm referring to virtually any device running the Android operating system that permits additional apps to be installed on it.

In fact, for this book I used no less than four different Android devices to evaluate the apps. Three of them were Android phones: a Samsung Epic 4G, HTC Incredible, and HTC Legend. But the fourth device was a 7-inch CherryPal CherryPad America (C515) tablet that doesn't have broadband Internet connectivity — just a Wi-Fi connection. For around the home or office (connected to a Wi-Fi router), the tablet worked fine with many of the apps, proving (at least to me) that Android is suited for far more than just mobile phones.

Many of the apps reviewed in this book are available from multiple sources and are just a Google search away. *All* of the apps reviewed are available from the Android Market, and I conveniently include a QR Code for each app next to the review that links directly to the app's entry in the Android Market.

 A QR Code is a funky-looking, square bar code that has embedded information that a scanner can read and interpret. If your Android device has a built-in camera and an installed app that can read QR Codes, all you need to do is fire up the app and point your device's camera at the QR Code. After the QR Code is successfully read, the bar code scanner app converts the embedded information into text; then it should launch the corresponding app on your device — which, in the case of the QR codes in this book, is the Android Market app. (My favorite free bar code scanner app in the Android Market is the appropriately named Barcode Scanner.)

I also list the prices for each app (as of when the book was printed). Sometimes app prices go up and sometimes they go down. In fact, paid apps sometimes become free apps and vice versa. Developers from all over the globe make their apps available in the Android Market, which is why you see some apps listed in different currencies, such as the euro (€) or pound sterling (£). The Android Market automatically converts the price of the apps into your local currency so that you can quickly gauge how much an app will cost without having to figure out currency conversion rates. But because currency values fluctuate wildly, I list app prices in this book in their native currencies. (When you purchase an app from the Android Market, you go though a series of pages. The final page you see before you commit to the purchase always shows the app's price in its native currency.)

How This Book Is Organized

Pick a page, any page, any page at all. Really. You don't need to start at the beginning and work your way through, page-by-page, to the very end. Just go straight to the chapter or review of the specific app that you want to learn more about. Think of this book as a reference guide to Amazing Android apps. As to why it's organized the way it is, I had to put the chapters in *some* order, so alphabetically seemed the best way to go . . .

. . . Except for the first chapter, "Understanding Android." It is the only one that doesn't actually *review* any Android apps. Chapter 1 discusses exactly what Android is and some of the ins-and-outs about Android apps in general. The remaining 18 chapters are all app reviews of: Books; Communications; Education and Children's Apps; Entertainment; Finance; Games; Health, Food, and Fitness; Music; News and Weather; Photography and Video; Productivity and Business; Reference; Shopping and Dining Out; Social Networking; Sports; Tools; Travel and Navigation; and Utilities.

Each chapter includes reviews of five apps, listed alphabetically, with each review getting two pages of description and screenshots. Following these reviews are another five reviews — also in alphabetical order — with shorter descriptions. The apps within each chapter are not ranked in any way. The longer reviews do not necessarily mean that they are better apps than the apps in the shorter reviews — it's just that for some apps there's more to talk about.

Icons Used in This Book

Throughout this book you see small icons located in the left margins. These icons are there to call your attention to an extra tidbit of information or offer some sage advice. Here are the icons you'll see in this book and what they mean:

These are suggestions, hints, and shortcuts that will help you wring even more usefulness out of the apps.

Sometimes it's good to know what's going on under the hood. While certainly not essential for using the apps, these extra morsels of information might give you a deeper appreciation for an app's inner workings — or at least perhaps impress your friends at your next dinner party with your newfound wisdom.

If everything worked exactly the way we expect it to, we wouldn't need *For Dummies* books, right? Pay attention when you see this icon, because I'm trying to save you from making a potential mistake that could cost you time, money, or embarrassment — or perhaps all three.

Where to Go from Here

Isn't it obvious? Fire up your Android device, launch the Android Market app, and start installing some apps!

1 Understanding Android

In mobile device terms, the word *Android* can refer to either an Android device or to the Android operating system. In very simple terms, an Android device is any device that runs the Android operating system. You might also encounter androids from science fiction films and books, which are robots that resemble people, but that's not the type of Android I discuss in this book.

You don't need to understand what Android is or how it works to use it. You can simply turn your device on and start pressing buttons and tapping icons and you'll probably get along just fine. That approach worked just fine for my 3-year-old daughter; she figured it out pretty quickly, much to my dismay. But in case you want a small peek behind the Android curtain, this chapter is for you . . .

Introducing the Android Operating System

Android is the operating system that powers all Android devices. Much like how the Windows operating system powers laptop and desktop computers, or Apple's iOS (formerly known as the iPhone OS) powers iPhones and iPads. Think of it as the underlying software that instructs your device what to do. When you install an Android app onto an Android device, you are installing an app that was written specifically for the Android operating system. You can't install a Windows app on an Android device, and you can't install an Android app onto a Windows computer.

Actually, that last part isn't exactly true. You actually *can* install Android apps onto a Windows computer — and even on Macs and Linux PCs, for that matter — but only if the computer is running a special piece of software called an Android *emulator,* which creates a virtual Android device on your computer. Developers frequently use such emulators to test their apps.

Speaking of Linux, the Android operating system is actually an offshoot of the Linux operating system. Since its inception, however, Android has developed into a robust, independent operating system designed for mobile devices, and it's not actually directly compatible with Linux.

Android is an *open source* operating system, which means that a large community of companies and developers maintain it and contribute toward developing newer versions of it. This all takes place under the auspices of Google, which bought the company (Android, Inc.) that first developed the Android OS. Unlike Apple's iOS operating system, the Android operating system's ongoing development isn't hidden behind lock and key. In fact, about 80 companies are members of the group — the Open Handset Alliance — that contribute towards the further development of the Android operating system.

Dealing with Fragmentation

All of this openness allows for innovation from many different sources. This also allows for many different Android devices to come in all shapes and sizes — which is great for you, as it gives you lots of options — but it creates a compatibility problem for the app developers. The compatibility issue is such a big problem with Android devices that it's even got a name: *fragmentation.*

Manufacturers are free to modify the Android operating system as they see fit for their devices. This allows the manufacturers a way to differentiate their Android devices from their competitors' devices, by adding unique features. But this also results in different customized versions of Android running on different devices. An example of this is that mobile phone maker HTC inserts its own HTC Sense user interface into many of its Android phones, whereas Samsung puts its own TouchWiz user interface into its Android devices. Figure 1-1 shows a couple of screens from my Samsung Epic 4G Android phone.

Manufacturers also control which version of the Android operating system powers their devices. For instance, when this book was printed, the latest version of Android was version 2.3, which has the nickname "Gingerbread." (All versions of the Android operating system are named after desserts. Maybe that explains why I always craved sweets while I was working on this book.)

Android 2.3 arrived at the tail end of 2010, but only a mere five months after the previous version, Android 2.2 ("Froyo" or "Frozen Yogurt") was released. At the end of 2010, despite that Android 2.2 had been available for months, it's estimated that only about 40 percent of all Android devices were running it, while another 40 percent of Android devices were still running Android 2.1 ("Éclair"). The rest were running even older versions, such as Android 1.6 ("Donut") or Android 1.5 ("Cupcake").

Just because an update to the operating system is available doesn't mean that a manufacturer is willing or ready to update a device's operating system. My Samsung Epic 4G was running Android 2.1 until early December 2010, when it finally upgraded to Android 2.2 (ironically, just a week before Android 2.3 was officially released). On the other hand, my HTC Incredible has been running Android 2.2 since August 2010 (see Figure 1-2).

Figure 1-1: My Samsung Epic 4G Android phone's home page (left) and one of the app pages (right).

Figure 1-2: My Samsung Epic 4G running Android 2.1 (left), and my HTC Incredible running Android 2.2 (right).

Another big differentiator between devices is the hardware that runs them. Some Android devices have big screens, fast processors, and lots of bells and whistles; other Android devices have tiny displays, slow CPUs, and very few extras. And there are plenty of Android devices that fall in between these two extremes.

All these differences between Android devices wind up creating huge headaches for app developers. They need to try to ensure compatibility on many different devices, using dissimilar hardware, running various versions of the Android operating system, and must take into account any customizations made to the Android operating system by the manufacturers.

The end result, as you might guess, is apps mayhem. In some cases, the apps simply won't run on some devices. Other times, the apps run, but certain features won't work. And in some instances, the apps appear to run fine for a few minutes, but then suddenly stop working. If you read the comments that users leave for the apps in the Android Market, you often see complaints about how some apps won't work on certain devices.

One of the most popular Android apps is the game Angry Birds. It was downloaded over 8 million times in just its first eight weeks. But it didn't come without a hitch. Many users complained that it wouldn't run on their devices, it ran too slowly, or it stopped working. Angry Birds' developer, Rovio Mobile, released several updates to address the compatibility problems, but numerous issues still remained with some devices.

After eight weeks, Rovio Mobile finally conceded on its blog: "Despite our efforts, we were unsuccessful in delivering optimal performance." Rovio Mobile went on to list a handful of Android devices that Angry Birds was known not to be compatible with, but promised that further updates should run better on more devices.

If you want to read more about Angry Birds, check out my review of it in Chapter 7.

Using Android on Devices Other Than Phones

Although the Android operating system is geared for use in mobile devices, this doesn't mean that all Android devices have to be mobile phones. Yes, the majority of Android devices on the market now are phones, but that's starting to change.

Android tablets are becoming increasingly popular, thanks in part to devices such as the 5-inch Dell Streak and the 7-inch Samsung Galaxy Tab (see Figure 1-3). Certainly the popularity of Apple's iPad tablet helped spark some healthy competition on the Android front. In fact, one of the devices I used to evaluate apps for this book was a tablet — the 7-inch CherryPal CherryPad America (C515).

Speaking of fragmentation of Android devices, of the three tablets I mention, the Dell Streak runs Android 1.6 (Donut), the CherryPal CherryPad America (C515) runs Android 2.1 (Éclair), and the Samsung Galaxy Tab runs Android 2.2 (Froyo). If that isn't enough, the Android operating system won't be truly *optimized* to run on tablets until the next version of Android ("Honeycomb"), which is due out sometime in 2011. Is your head spinning yet?

Figure 1-3: The Samsung Galaxy Tab Android tablet.

The Android OS powers some portable media players as well, such as the popular Archos 7 home tablet. And let's not forget about e-readers. Barnes & Noble's Nook e-reader device also happens to be powered by the Android operating system.

But before you get too excited about all of these Android devices, I need to reel things back in again, in light of what this book is all about — Android apps. As it just so happens, neither the Archos 7 home tablet nor the Barnes & Noble Nook can access the Android Market. This doesn't mean that it's impossible to install Android apps on these devices, but doing so involves more convoluted means or outright hacking the devices beyond the manufacturers' intent.

Which brings me to . . .

Shopping at the Android Market

Every app that's reviewed in this book is available from the Android Market. Many of these apps are available from other sources as well, which I get to shortly.

First and foremost, the Android Market is an *app* that comes preinstalled on most Android devices. You can see the icon for the Market app on the home page of my Samsung Epic 4G in Figure 1-1. Fire up the Market app and you can search and browse for apps to install on your device.

Figure 1-4 shows what the Android Market looks like. The image on the left displays what some of the top-paid apps were when I took the screenshot. You can also see the top free apps, apps that were just added to the Market, as well as apps and games by category. Tap the magnifying glass button in the upper-right corner to search for apps by their name, developer, or description.

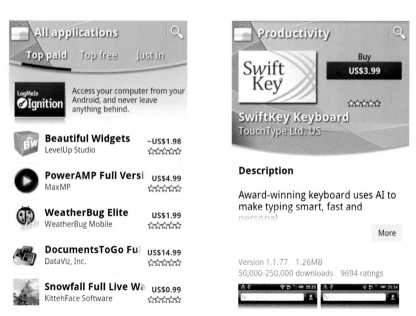

Figure 1-4: Top-paid apps in the Android Market (left); the description page for the SwiftKey Keyboard app (right).

Look closely at the image on the left and you see a tilde character (~) in front of the price for the Beautiful Widgets app. The tilde means that the listed price is approximate. Some apps are sold in currencies other than the U.S. dollar. In the case of Beautiful Widgets, its actual price is €1.49 (1 euro and 49 cents). The Android Market automatically converts the prices of paid apps to your native currency.

Tap the entry of an app in the list to open the description of the app, such as is in the image on the right in Figure 1-4. The description page for an app usually includes an explanation of what the app does, some of its key features, and a couple of screenshots of the app in action. Sometimes you also see information about recent changes or updates, and mentions of other versions of the app, such as trial and pro versions. The version number of the app is provided, as are the size of the app (in KB or MB), and how many times the app has been downloaded. You also find links to see more apps in the Market from the developer, the developer's Web page, and the developer's e-mail address. The very bottom of the page includes a link for you to flag the app as inappropriate, if you feel it contains objectionable content.

There's also a reviews section where you can see comments that users have posted about the app, such as in the image on the left in Figure 1-5. The most recent comments appear at the top of the page; scroll down to see older comments. Every comment also includes a user rating from one to five stars. The average of all the user ratings appears at the top of the page.

Figure 1-5: The user comments page for the Evernote app (left); the parts of your device that the Facebook can access (right).

Installing apps

If you come across a free app that you want to install, tap the Install button that appears at the top of the app's description page. A new page appears, which lists your device's services that the app can access. For example, the image on the right in Figure 1-5 shows that the Facebook app can access a device's system tools, Internet access, stored personal information, and account information. If you're okay with all this, tap the OK button and the app will install. If not, tap the back button and go find another app.

Before you can access the Android Market, you first have to link your device to a Google account — even if all you want to do is install only free apps. If your device isn't already linked to a Google account and you try to launch the Market app, a page appears that will walk you through linking your device or creating a new Google account. To create a Google account, you need to provide your first and last names and pick a username and password.

Purchasing apps

Remember, some apps cost money. If you want to purchase a paid app, tap the Buy button that appears at the top of the app's description page (refer to Figure 1-4). If the app accesses any services on your device, you'll next see a page informing you what the app will have access to (refer to Figure 1-5). Tap OK on this page and the next page you see is the Google Checkout page (see Figure 1-6)

When this book was printed, the *only* way you could pay for apps in the Android Market was to use the Google Checkout payment service. In the U.S., Google Checkout links your Google account to an American Express, Discover, MasterCard, or Visa account. (If you are a T-Mobile customer, you can also link your Google Checkout account to bill you through T-Mobile.) Outside the U.S., you can link Google Checkout to Solo and Visa Electron accounts. The rumor mills were whispering, however, that it's just a matter of time before additional payment options, such as PayPal, get added to the Android Market.

If your payment information isn't already in Google Checkout, enter it from this page. If your payment info is already in Google Checkout, then as soon as you tap the Buy Now button, you authorize the purchase and the app will be downloaded and installed to your device. If the app is priced using a currency other than your native currency (see the image on the left in Figure 1-7), you see the *actual* price here — be it in U.S. dollars, pound sterling, or euros (see the image on the right in Figure 1-7).

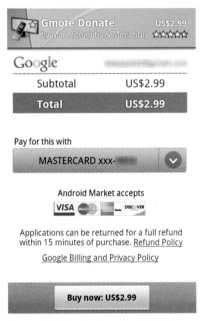

Figure 1-6: Google Checkout (left). Purchase an app a second time (after a refund) and no more refunds are allowed (right).

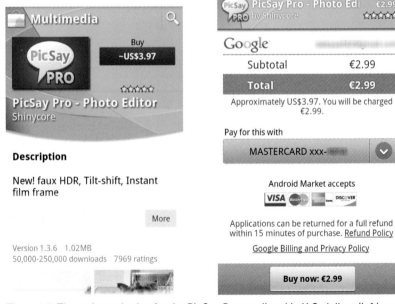

Figure 1-7: The estimated price for the PicSay Pro app listed in U.S. dollars (left); app prices show in their native currency (right) at time of purchase.

One nifty feature of the Android market is that you can choose to return an app for a full refund. Google recently reduced this grace period from 24 hours to 15 minutes, however, so you better decide quickly if you want to keep that app you just purchased.

If your return a paid app for a refund and then later decide that you want to install it again, you no longer are eligible for the grace period (refer to Figure 1-6). If you buy an app for a second time, it's going to be a keeper.

If you keep an app for longer than the grace period, it's yours forever. You can uninstall it and choose to reinstall it months later — even if your device gets completely reset or replaced by a new device. To do this, however, the device must be linked to the same Google account that you used to initially purchase the app.

Buying from Other App Stores

The Android Market isn't the only Android app store in town. Here's a handful of Web sites from which you can also download and install free and paid Android apps directly onto your device. For some, you can download apps directly from the sites using your device's Web browser, whereas for others you need to download the sites' own app-store apps:

- ✔ **AndroidPit:** `androidpit.com`
- ✔ **Appoke:** `appoke.com`
- ✔ **GetJar:** `m.getjar.com` (see Figure 1-8)
- ✔ **Handango:** `m.handango.com`
- ✔ **SlideMe Marketplace:** `m.slideme.org`

Many sites enable you to download Android apps onto your computer first and then transfer them to your Android device. Installing an app this way is commonly referred to as *sideloading*. This topic is a bit too advanced for this book, but you can find plenty of details and instructions online for how to do this.

Before you can install Android apps that come from sources other than the Android Market onto your device, you must set your device to permit the installation of non-Market apps. Configure this in your device's settings under Applications (see Figure 1-8).

Android vs. iPhone

Would any discussion of Android be complete without drawing a comparison of it to the iPhone and related devices (such as the iPad and iPod touch)? At their cores, they are similar devices. They're both mobile platforms with infrastructures in place to run free and paid third-party apps that greatly increase the functionality of the devices.

I'm frequently asked which is better, the iPhone or Android? Despite my obvious allegiance to Android, I don't necessarily declare Android the hands-down winner. The way I see it, it's a matter of personal preference — much like how some folks prefer Windows computers and some prefer Macs. Being the uber-geek that I am, I have Android devices *and* I have an iPhone. I also have both Windows and Mac computers. You can call me the *techno-diplomat*.

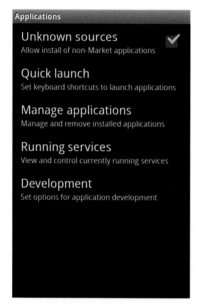 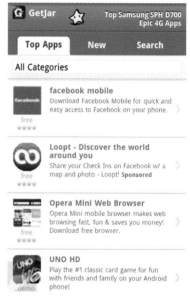

Figure 1-8: Enable the installation of non-Market apps in your device's settings (left). GetJar is an excellent non-Market source for Android apps (right).

Figure 1-9: The iPhone version of WeatherBug Elite app (left), and the Android version (right).

Of course, there are some inherent differences between the iPhone and Android devices, and advocates for both sides will be quick to launch a smear campaign against the other camp. Some accuse Android of not being as secure a platform as the iPhone. Some accuse Apple of stifling innovation by taking such a heavy-handed approach with policing its App Store. Some think Google is far too liberal with how it manages the apps allowed into the Android Market. Some argue that limiting the iPhone to specific service providers is tantamount to giving Apple a virtual monopoly. And so on . . .

You also find many apps that are available for *both* platforms. In some cases, the two versions look and act very similarly. In other cases, the differences are obvious. For instance, the iPhone and Android versions of the WeatherBug Elite app are side-by-side in Figure 1-9. They look different, but which one is better?

So, no, I'm not going to answer any of the questions about which platform, or which app, or which operating system, or which device is better. They're both pretty darn amazing if you ask me! But don't take my word for it —get your hands on an iPhone and try it out. Then spend some time with an Android device and put it through the paces. And while you're at it, why don't you try some of the apps in this book?

2 Books

 Aldiko Book Reader
Free (ad supported)

When it comes to electronic book (e-book) readers, the first name that probably comes to mind is Amazon's Kindle. Kindle deserves its solid reputation, and I review the Kindle for Android app later in this chapter. But as easy-to-use as Kindle for Android is, and despite the vast selection of e-books in the Kindle Store, you have to pry open your wallet if you want to read the majority of the available Kindle books.

Aldiko Book Reader offers a similar elegant-looking interface and is equally easy to use. The difference, however, is that Aldiko Book Reader offers access to a much larger library of *free* e-books than Kindle for Android does.

 Before you get too excited about the prospect of reading thousands of free e-books, note that most of them are books in the public domain. In other words, many of these are old books — you won't find any recent *New York Times* bestsellers here. But you will find plenty of classics, including many books that are often required reading for high school students. It doesn't include only books that were written before you were born, however. You can also download recent self-published books from new authors. And there are even a few options to purchase recent tech and romance titles, as well as inexpensive selections from independent authors and publishers.

While reading, you have a lot of control over how the pages look. You can set the font type, size, and weight. You can change the line spacing, horizontal and vertical margins, and even the text alignment. You can also set the background and font colors for daytime and nighttime reading modes. A preview of how the page will look appears at the top of the settings screen, so you won't be in for any rude surprises the next time you open an e-book.

Aldiko Book Reader lets you customize some of its navigation controls. You can set what happens when you swipe left, right, upward, and downward. The options are to turn to the next page, turn to the preceding page, or do nothing.

To skip ahead or behind to another section of the book, call up the table of contents and tap the entry for the chapter you want to go to. You can also set bookmarks and then later jump directly to any of the pages you bookmarked. You can also search for words within a book, and Aldiko Book Reader provides a list of all the places where that word appears. Tap an entry in the search results to go directly to that page.

Although Aldiko Book Reader is ad supported, you never see the ads while you are reading a book. In fact, the ads appear only on the Download Books screens. To banish the ads completely, purchase Aldiko Book Reader Premium for $2.99 from the Android Market.

Best features

You can import into Aldiko Book Reader any e-book that is saved in the common ePub file format.

Worst features

If you want to read a book from the bestseller list, Aldiko Book Reader isn't going to do you much good. For that you're going to need Kindle for Android.

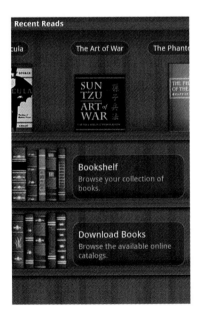

Chapter **1**

Loomings

Call me Ishmael. Some years ago— never mind how long precisely— having little or no money in my purse, and nothing particular to interest me on shore, I thought I would sail about a little and see the watery part of the world. It is a way I have of driving off the spleen and regulating the circulation. Whenever I find myself growing grim about the mouth; whenever it is a damp, drizzly November in my soul; whenever I find myself involuntarily pausing before

Audible for Android

Free

As much as I love reading, I often don't have the time to sit down and engross myself in a good book. I'm frequently too busy during the day and often too tired at night. And I know I'm not the only working parent who feels this way. Books should be read far more frequently than just once or twice a year while on vacation. It's quite a predicament for a bibliophile.

But thanks to Audible for Android's plethora of current audio books to choose from, I can squeeze in my book time while I'm commuting or even showering. And as much as I thought I was a reading purist (some might go so far as to call me a snob), I enjoy hearing books professionally narrated — often by the books' very own authors.

In order to download and listen to Audible's audio books, you first have to become an Audible.com member. Memberships start at $14.95 per month, which entitles you to one audio book download per month. When you first install Audible for Android, you have the option of trying out the app without being a member; you can download and listen to a number of audio book samples to help you decide if you want to sign up.

Audible for Android shares similar traits with traditional e-book readers, such as the capability to create bookmarks and skip to the next or preceding chapters. It even has a "Button-Free" mode that lets you tap the screen to play and pause, and swipe left or right to rewind or fast-forward 30 seconds.

Because this is an audio-based app, Audible for Android also includes a number of audio-specific features, such as pause, rewind, and fast-forward. Audible for Android supports multitasking, so you can exit out of the app to check e-mail or surf the Web while you continue listening to an audio book. Tap the "Back 30 Button" to instantly rewind the audio 30 seconds. The settings enable you to customize this time to anywhere between 1 and 300 seconds — despite what you set it to, though, the button's icon always shows the number 30 on it (see the figure on the right).

If you like to be lulled to sleep with a good story, Audible for Android includes a Sleep Mode that automatically stops playback after 15, 30, 45, or 60 minutes. You could relive your childhood and fall asleep to Dr. Seuss or Winnie the Pooh.

Purchase audio books directly from within the Audible for Android app, from a computer's Web browser, or from another Audible-enabled device. All of your purchased audio books are permanently stored in Audible.com's online library, and you need only download the audio books you plan on listening to any given time. As long as your subscription is active, you can re-download any of your purchased audio books on any supported device. (You can access your account from up to four computers and three mobile devices.)

Best features

Audible for Android's best feature is its extensive selection of audio books that span a wide array of genres. You even find current *New York Times* bestsellers available for your listening enjoyment.

Worst features

This review is based on the first version of Audible for Android, which plays audio only at normal speed. Many users — myself included — would love the capability to play audio at slower (half) or faster (2x) speeds. Audible promises that adding this feature is in the works, and it might be in place by the time you read this.

Books WordPlayer
Free

Books WordPlayer is an e-book reader that isn't as polished or easy to use as the popular Aldiko Book Reader or Kindle for Amazon apps (both of which I review in this chapter). But don't write off Books WordPlayer simply because it isn't as pretty as the other e-book readers; it has several tricks up its sleeve that the other e-book reader apps lack.

Before I get into what makes Books WordPlayer so special, I want to assure you that it is very much a capable e-book reader, even without all the bells and whistles. You can control how a book's pages appear on the screen by adjusting things like the text and background colors. You also have several options for how the text looks, with settings for the font type, size, and spacing. You can create bookmarks, search for text within a book, and customize how taps and swipes move forward and backward through the book.

But what is quite possibly Books WordPlayer's most outstanding feature is its Speak Chapter feature, which reads aloud the text of a book. Why read a book when it can be read to you? This uses your Android device's text-to-speech functionality, so the audio quality is not going to be anywhere as near as polished as the professionally recorded narrations by top Hollywood actors, like you find with Audible's audio books (also reviewed in this chapter). Books WordPlayer reads text with a dry, obviously artificial voice. But if you have to get behind the wheel of your car and just can't put down the e-book you're engrossed in, this is a great way to find out sooner than later if the butler really did do it.

 When you first attempt to use Books WordPlayer's speech feature, it prompts you that it needs to install the free Speech for WordPlayer helper application. Tap OK to automatically load the page for the app in the Android Market so you can install it.

You can add books to Books WordPlayer's library three different ways (see the figure on the left). One way is to simply load ePub files from your device's SD Card. This means, of course, that you first have to get the files into your device's SD Card by either downloading them or transferring them over from your computer.

If you are an e-book aficionado and have an extensive library of e-books, you should check out the free Calibre e-book management software (www.calibre-ebook.com), which helps you manage all your e-books on your computer — and it can even convert many other e-book file formats into ePub files. If you use Calibre, Books WordPlayer can communicate with it over your wireless network, and use this connection to add books to Books WordPlayer's library on your device.

You can also add free books to Books WordPlayer's library by downloading them from a wide selection of free online sources. As with Aldiko Book Reader, these titles are older public-domain works or independently published works.

Best features

Believe it or not, Books WordPlayer has access to millions of free book titles from online sources. With just a few taps, you can download books from Google Books, Smashwords, or Feedbooks (see the figure on the right).

Worst features

The user interface is awkward and it isn't easy to navigate to a specific part of a book unless it's the beginning of a chapter or you previously created a bookmark for that section.

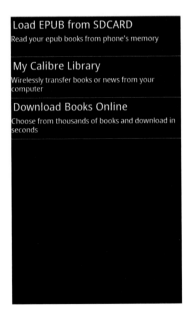

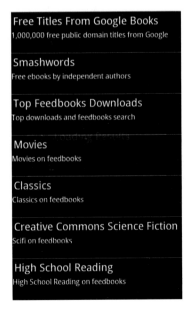

Droid Comic Viewer
Free

The big names in comic books — namely, DC Comics and Marvel — have yet to grace Android devices with digital versions of their comic books. You can read their digital comics on your computer, iPhone, or iPad, but not the very device to which this book is devoted. But DC Comics and Marvel aren't the only comic book games in town. Smaller, independent comic book publishing companies are producing more universally available digital comics, and a community of users is devoted to converting older, public domain comics into digital versions that can be viewed on a wide range of devices.

Mobile-comic publisher Robot Comics recognized that there wasn't a decent comic book viewer app for Android devices, and took it upon itself to create one. The result is Droid Comic Viewer (also known as ACV), which is probably the most versatile Android comic book viewing app available.

Droid Comic Viewer can read popular digital comic book formats, such as CBR and CBZ files. A number of online sites, such as flash backuniverse.com and fawcettcomic.com, offer free, legal CBR downloads. The latter of those sites hosts a growing collection of titles from the '40s and '50s, such as *Captain Marvel* and *Plastic Man*. Droid Comic Viewer can read image folders that contain JPEG, PNG, BMP, and GIF files. Files are stored on your device's SD card.

Droid Comic Viewer also reads comics that use the open-source ACV and ACV2 file formats. Not coincidentally, Robot Comics offers a large selection of ACV comics in the Android Market — many of which are free (search for "Robot Comics" in the Android Market).

Navigating through comic books is rather intuitive, as the app supports typical gestures, such as pinch to zoom, and swipe to move forward and backward. All of the controls are highly customizable; you can set what happens for individual gestures like double-tap, swipe up, and tap the screen's top-right corner —to mention a few. A "Reading direction" setting controls whether the comic goes from left-to-right or from right-to-left (which is common for Japanese manga).

View comic books in either landscape or portrait mode with just the tap of a button — or set the display to auto-rotate if you don't want to lock in a specific orientation. Positioned in the bottom corners of the screen is a pair of transparent buttons that change the view to the next or preceding page. If you want, make these buttons invisible — just tap the part of the screen where the buttons would ordinarily show up and the page will turn accordingly.

If a comic is especially long, you might want to enable the setting that shows screen numbers, so you can better gauge where you are in the comic book. A Browse button lets you navigate through comic books based on thumbnail images of the pages. Not all comic books have thumbnails, so you might instead just see blank boxes when you use the Browse feature.

Best features

If you stop reading a comic book while still in the middle of it, Droid Comic Viewer remembers what page you were looking at when you quit. The next time you open that comic book, it opens to the page where you left off.

Worst features

You can't create bookmarks, like you can with most e-book readers.

Kindle for Android
Free

With nearly instant access to more than 750,000 e-books, Kindle for Android could very possibly make you the smartest person you know — or at least the most well read! And I'm not talking about just any old books here, but everything from just-published works, to *New York Times* bestsellers, to the classics, and more. Best yet, many of these works cost significantly less than their hardcover and soft-cover versions. Numerous older works that are in the public domain are even available cost free!

Kindle is the e-book platform that Amazon launched in late 2007 with its dedicated e-book Kindle device. Since then, Amazon not only has released updated versions of the device, but also has made Kindle e-book reading software available for numerous mobile platforms, such as the iPhone, BlackBerry, and Android. You don't actually need a Kindle to read a Kindle e-book.

Even if you own a Kindle, you can still access all of your purchased e-books from your Android device with Kindle for Android — which comes in mighty handy when you want to pick up where you left off in that whodunit, but you don't have your Kindle with you. Kindle for Android will even tell you the last page you read, regardless of which device you were using to read the book (see the figure on the right). Kindle for Android also allows you to add bookmarks and notes, and highlight sections of a page, and these will all sync to any other device you use to read that book. You can even select any word that appears in a book and look up its meaning in Dictionary.com and Wikipedia.

 You may find reading a book on the relatively small-size screen of a device like an Android phone to be too trying, but Kindle for Android has a few options that make it easier to read. Choose from three back-ground colors and five text sizes. You can also view books in land-scape mode. When in landscape mode, tap the little padlock icon that appears in the lower-right corner to lock the screen's orientation.

Kindle for Android offers several options to navigate through a book's pages. To move back and forth a page at a time, swipe the screen in the appropriate direction or tap the page's margin. If you briefly tap the middle of a page, a scroll bar appears at the bottom of the page and lets you quickly zip to any page in the book. A Go To option enables you to jump to a book's cover, table of contents, first chapter, a specific loca-tion, or even to your own notes, highlights, and bookmarks.

You can search within a book for a particular word or phrase. The results screen shows how many times that word or phrase appears and includes a brief excerpt from each occurrence. Tap on any result and Kindle for Android instantly jumps to that page in the book. And in case you are wondering, Kindle for Android reports that the word "Carpathian" appears in *Dracula* nine times.

Best features

You can "sample" many of the offerings from the Kindle Store for free. These samples typically include a book's cover, its table of contents, and the first couple of chapters.

Worst features

You can't add any books to your Kindle account — be they purchases, samples, or otherwise — directly from within the Kindle for Android app. You first have to add the book to your account from the Kindle Store using a Web browser (on your device or a computer) before they show up in Kindle for Android.

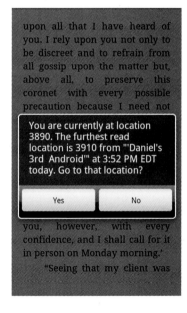

Bible.is
Free

Bible.is is truly one of the most universal apps I've come across. It offers multiple versions of the Old and New Testaments in many languages. In addition to text, many of the versions also include professionally recorded narration with dramatic readings and music soundtracks.

You can easily navigate through a Bible's books and chapters using Bible.is's intuitive table of contents. One chapter appears onscreen at a time, but you can easily move forward or backward by swiping the right or left edges of the display. You can bookmark passages and share them on Facebook, if you feel inspired. Bible.is even offers a number of suggested "Programs" for Bible study readings.

Book Catalogue
Free

Many reviews in this chapter are about apps for reading books *on* your device. Lest you think I overlooked physical books, this app's for you. For avid readers who quickly accumulate a large library of books, Book Catalogue helps tame your seemingly unmanageable book collection.

You *could* add books by typing in all the relevant information, but it's far easier if you let Book Catalogue look up the information for you, by scanning in the book's barcode or by typing in the book's ISBN. Book Catalogue gets this information from Google Books, including thumbnails of book covers. You can also add your own comments to an entry, as well as track when you start and finish reading a book. You can even track who borrows your books.

DailyStrip
Free (ad supported)

Whether you are a *Doonesbury* fan or prefer the likes of *Beetle Bailey*, chances are your favorite daily comic strips are amongst the 140 different strips that you can view with DailyStrip. You can view the current day's strips or see ones from past dates. While DailyStrip can go only so far back in time for some strips, I used the app to read the very first published *Dilbert* from April 16, 1989.

You can set your favorite comic strip as the default strip, so that it automatically appears, showing the current day's strip, when you launch DailyStrip. You can also add strips to a list of favorites, making it easier to go straight to the ones you like. If a particular day's strip tickles your fancy, you can bookmark it, share a link to it with your friends, or save it as a JPEG to your device's SD card. I could go on, but I need to get back to catching up with *Mother Goose and Grimm.*

 ## Okenko Books Reader
Free

There's no reason why *you* should have all the fun with your Android device — why not let the family join in as well? Gather your 4- to 8-year-olds and cozy up to some e-books for kids with Okenko Books Reader ("Okenko" is Czech for "small window").

Okenko Books Reader is a subscription service that publishes a new children's book every two weeks. Subscriptions start at $2 per month, and you get access to all previously published books as well as new ones. When you install the app, it includes one free book, so you can get a taste first without having to commit to a subscription.

All of the books are from first-time children's book authors. Each month, a short, illustrated book is published, suited for younger children. About two weeks later, a longer work that contains more text comes out, which is geared toward kids who have already started reading.

 ## TinyComics
Free

With TinyComics, you might never again have to pester your local comic book shop owner about when the next issue of *Adventure Comics* is due to hit the stands. TinyComics tracks the release dates for comic books from the major publishers for the current and coming weeks. Each comic listed includes a thumbnail image of the cover, a description of the issue, and its cover price.

If you're interested in some of the smaller or independent comic book publishers, check out the Comic Shopper app instead (free in the Android Market). It displays only the current and next week's releases, and it doesn't include thumbnails or issue descriptions, but its list of comic book titles is more extensive.

3 Communications

 Dolphin Browser HD
Free (ad supported)

Dolphin Browser HD is one of the most powerful Web browsers available for Android devices. And that's saying a lot, because there are many available browser options, including the popular (and free) Firefox and Opera Mini browsers.

 TIP You can install multiple browsers on your Android device. Consider doing this if you want to see which one suits your needs the best. Some frequently visited sites may work better with some browsers than with others. Two additional browser apps you might want to check out are Skyfire Browser and xScope Browser.

Dolphin Browser HD features a minimalist interface that provides maximum space for displaying pages. At the top of the screen are tabs for each Web page you have open — you can have up to eight pages open at once. The tabs scroll left and right so you can easily see which pages are open. Below the tabs are an address bar, a home-page button, and a page refresh button. As soon as you start scrolling down a page, all these items disappear, enabling the page to fill the entire screen.

Swipe the page to the right and your bookmarks appear in a window pane on the left side of the screen (see the figure on the left). Swipe the page to the left to open the add-on toolbar in a pane on the right. Yes, I said "add-on." Dolphin Browser HD supports a growing collection of third-party add-ons that add functionality to the browser for doing things like managing your passwords and saving Web pages as PDFs. Some of these add-ons are themes that let you change the way Dolphin Browser HD looks.

Like most Android browsers, Dolphin Browser HD supports multi-touch pinch functionality for zooming into pages. Dolphin Browser HD also includes a mobile-view feature that lets you see Web pages in a much simpler layout, without pictures or ads. If you tap and hold the address bar, a pop-up window gives you options, such as adding the current page as a bookmark, searching for text on the page, and saving a local copy of the page.

As soon as you venture into Dolphin Browser HD's settings, the sheer number of settings you can control will probably take you aback. There's nowhere near enough room here to cover them all, but trust me when I tell you if there's a browser setting you want to control, Dolphin Browser HD probably lets you do it.

Best features

The coolest part of Dolphin Browser HD is its gesture commands. Tap the Gesture button in the bottom-left corner of the screen to trace a gesture on the screen that acts as a shortcut. For instance, a preset gesture lets you trace the letter "G" on the screen to launch www.google.com, or tracing an upward-facing arrow jumps to the top of the current page (see the figure on the right). You can even create your own custom gestures.

Worst features

In an earlier iteration of Dolphin Browser HD, the app could sync its bookmarks with Google Bookmarks. That feature is no longer built into Dolphin Browser HD. Not all hope is lost, however, as you can regain that functionality by installing and configuring the Bookmarks to SD add-in.

fring
Free (ad supported)

If your Android device happens to be a relatively new smartphone, it likely includes a front-facing camera. The purpose of the camera is not to help you put your makeup on (although, I suppose you could do that if you wanted to), but so that you can send video of yourself to someone you are having a video call with. (There are times, however, when you may not want to do this — for instance, I work from home and often don't make it out of my pajamas until midday, so for any video calls I conduct, the camera always stays above my neck.)

Video calls might seem like a novelty, but many businesses rely on these face-to-face interactions when being there in person isn't feasible. Video calls are also a great way for family members to stay connected when they're separated by long distances. There are a number of decent video calling apps for Android devices, including the free Skype and Tango Video apps. The one that has the best overall feature set is fring. (That being said, Tango Video is probably the easiest to use, and I review it later in this chapter.)

With fring, not only can you conduct free video and voice calls with other fring users — or "fringsters" (there are also versions of fring for the iPhone and some Nokia phones) — but you can also have free voice calls with MSN Messenger and Google Talk users. You can also exchange instant messages with all of these users, as well as users who use AIM, ICQ, and Yahoo! instant messaging clients.

 When you first install fring, you can communicate only with other fringsters. You need to install add-ons (via Menu⇨Add-ons) to add access to users of these other services. Also, the quality of your call is dependent on the quality of the connection on both ends of the conversation. You experience better quality over Wi-Fi connections, but fring also works over Edge, 3G, and 4G connections. (Below you can see an example from a fring video call I had with my cat. She looks a little bored.) I advise against using fring's speakerphone feature; you'll likely experience annoying pauses and delays. For video calls, it's best to use a headset for the audio portion of the call.

fring taps into your address book and automatically identifies which users it can communicate with. It even displays which users are available to receive calls, busy, not available, or offline. Connecting to someone is as simple as selecting his or her name from fring's address book and then tapping the Chat, Call, or Video Call button. If you call people using a means that their service doesn't support, such as video calling, fring informs you of this fact.

By default, fring automatically fires itself up and runs in the background whenever your device starts up. As long as you don't quit fring (be careful if you use a Task Manager app, like SystemPanel, which I discuss in the Tools chapter), you'll be able to receive chats, voice calls, and video calls from other users.

Around the time I wrote this, fring had just come out with its fringOut service, which lets you use fring to make inexpensive international voice calls to landlines (also known as "real" phones) and mobile phones. Depending on where you are calling from and to, these calls can be as cheap as one cent per minute — such as domestic calls made within the U.S. (But if you call Scott Base in Antarctica, it will cost you $1.82 per minute.) I didn't have a chance to try fringOut, but I encountered a number of online users complaining about call quality. If you plan on using fringOut, do a little online research to see if these fresh-out-of-the-gate problems have been resolved.

Best features

Free video and voice calls . . . What's not to love?

Worst features

There's no way to tell when you've missed a voice or video call.

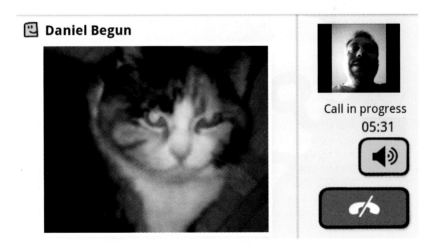

Google Voice
Free

The main tenet of Google Voice is that it gives you a single phone number that people can use to reach you, no matter which of your many phones (mobile, work, home) you happen to have access to at the moment. After you sign up for a free Google Voice phone number (at `www.google.com/voice`), you then input all your existing phone numbers that you want Google Voice to forward to when someone calls your Google Voice number. What this means is that when someone calls your Google Voice number, all your phones will ring simultaneously, and you can answer the call from any of these phones. If any of those phones are mobile phones, you'll also be able to receive text messages on them as well. None of this has any impact on the existing service of these phones — anyone calling those phones directly will still be able to get through.

You can enable and disable which phones Google Voice forwards to, whenever you want. You can even create a preset schedule for each phone for when Google Voice will forward to it — for instance, you can set Google Voice to forward to your work phone only between the hours of 9 a.m. and 5 p.m.

 Google Voice is a *service* provided by Google. Yes, it's an Android app too, but the Google Voice app is mostly just a conduit to accessing some of the service's features and settings. Technically, you could avail yourself of nearly everything that the Google Voice service offers without ever installing the Google Voice app. But using the Google Voice app makes it much easier to hear and read your voicemails and send and receive free texts. That said, to truly set up the Google Voice service to work exactly the way you want it to behave, you should do this on the Google Voice page first via a Web browser. Many of the settings I discuss here must be made via the Web and can't be done from within the app.

When people who aren't already in your contacts call your Google Voice number, they're asked to identify themselves. Then when your phone rings and you pick up, an automated voice tells you who is calling and gives you the option of either answering the call or sending it to voicemail. (You can disable this feature and instead have incoming calls directly connect as soon as you answer.) If you choose to send the call to voicemail, don't hang up quite yet, because you get to listen in on the message that the caller is leaving! If you then decide that you actually want to speak with the caller, press the * (asterisk) key to take the call.

Call screening goes a step further. For each person in your Google Contacts, you can create custom greetings, set which phones will ring when they call, send their calls directly to voicemail, or even block their calls.

There's plenty more Google Voice can do, but as you see, I've just about run out of space. Here are some final tidbits on what else you can do with Google Voice: Record phone conversations, get text and e-mail notifications of voicemails and missed calls, and make inexpensive international phone calls.

Best features

Google Voice automatically converts voicemail messages into text! The transcriptions might not always be letter perfect (see the figure on the right), but you can usually figure it out.

Worst features

Being able to send and receive free texts (SMS texts) is great, but you can't use Google Voice to send or receive messages that include photos or videos (MMS texts).

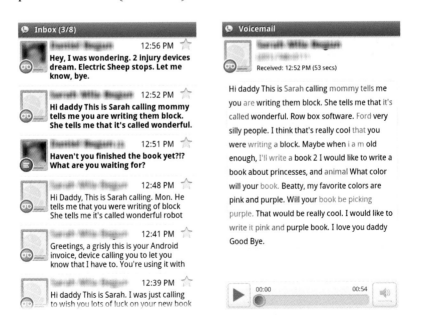

 **K-9 Mail**
Free

If you are a one-e-mail–address type of person who has simple e-mail needs, then any number of the Android e-mail apps should suffice. But for the rest of us who juggle multiple e-mail accounts, reply, forward, and send numerous e-mails throughout the day, K-9 Mail is the Android app of choice to get the job done.

K-9 Mail can access any combination of IMAP, POP3, and WebDAV (Exchange) e-mail accounts. All accounts appear on K-9 Mail's main screen, with the number of unread messages appearing to the right of each account (see the figure on the left). Tap any account to see all the messages that are sitting in that account's inbox. Messages that have attachments are highlighted; you can open attachments (assuming that your device has an app that supports the file type) or save them to your device's SD card.

When you open a message to read it, you can reply, reply to all, forward, or delete it. If the account supports it (such as GMail does), you can also archive the message, move it to another folder, or send it to a spam folder. At the bottom of every message are up and down arrows that navigate to the preceding or next e-mail in the inbox.

Instead of opening each account's inbox individually, you can use K-9 Mail's Integrated Inbox view to see the all messages sitting in the inboxes of all of your accounts on a single screen. You can sort by date, subject, sender, star, read/unread, or attachments. You can set each account to a different color, which appears on the left side of the screen, so you can quickly glean which account the individual e-mails are from (see the figure on the right). Also, if you're looking for a specific e-mail, but can't remember which account it's from, K-9 Mail can search through *all* of the accounts.

While K-9 Mail includes a number of global settings that control how it looks and acts, the app also includes detailed configuration settings for the individual e-mail accounts, so you can set different attributes for each account. Just some of the many available account settings are how frequently K-9 Mail automatically checks for new messages (this is commonly referred to as "push mail," as new mail is "pushed" out to K-9 Mail's inbox), how far back in time K-9 Mail should sync messages, and how much of each message K-9 Mail should automatically download (from 1KB to 2MB).

You can set up individual signatures for each account, and even designate one account as the default account for sending e-mails. You can also configure notifications for each account for when new messages arrive, including notifications on the status bar, vibrating the device, playing a different ringtone for each account, and even lighting the LED with a different color (if your device supports it).

If security is a top priority for you, K-9 Mail supports the OpenPGP data encryption standard. To use it, you also need to install the free APG app from the Android Market.

K-9 Mail includes several settings that make it easier to manage your e-mail after you're back in front of your main PC — such as whether to delete messages on the server when you delete them in K-9 Mail, and the option to always BCC yourself on any messages you send from K-9 Mail.

Best features

Bar none, K-9 Mail is the best e-mail app available for Android devices. Its advanced feature set even makes it a great candidate for use in corporate environments . . .

Worst features

. . . But only as long as your company's e-mail server isn't running Microsoft Exchange Server 2010, which doesn't support the WebDAV protocol. K-9 Mail also doesn't play nice with free Hotmail accounts.

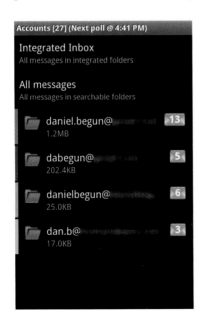

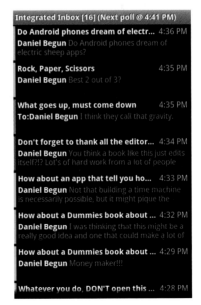

 **Visual VoiceMail**
Free (ad supported)

Back in days of yore, when knights and fair maidens received voicemail on their mobile phones, the only way they knew that they had voicemail waiting for them was if they noticed a voicemail icon on their phone's screen — if they were lucky, it also showed how many messages were waiting. They then had to call into voicemail, key in a passcode, and maneuver through the clunky voice prompts to listen to their messages. Okay, maybe it wasn't that long ago, but it feels that way.

These days, many smartphones use visual voicemail, which displays a list of all your voicemail messages, who left the messages, and when they were left. Tap an entry and the message plays. Not every smartphone has visual voicemail, and implementation often doesn't go beyond these features. But if your smartphone happens to be an Android device, the Visual VoiceMail app (also known as PhoneFusion Voicemail+) can do this and much more.

Visual VoiceMail replaces your phone's voicemail service with service provided by PhoneFusion. When you set up the Visual VoiceMail app, it should automatically make this switch for you. If not, you need to call into your phone's voicemail and manually forward it to PhoneFusion's voicemail number (813-200-0200 in the U.S.). Note that some carriers charge to forward voicemail.

After you install Visual VoiceMail, you can configure it to send you e-mail notifications when someone leaves you a voicemail or you missed a call (which is when someone listens to your outgoing message, but hangs up instead of leaving a message). You can also set Visual VoiceMail to play a notification sound and flash the LED when a voicemail arrives. I say "arrives" because the voicemail message is automatically downloaded to your device.

In the list of voicemails (see the figure on the left), messages you haven't listened to yet are highlighted in green. Long-tap a message to see your options for that message. These options include playing the voicemail, deleting it, forwarding it to an e-mail address or phone number, returning the call, sending an SMS message to the caller, and viewing the caller's contact information.

In addition to managing your voicemail, another cool thing Visual VoiceMail can do is receive faxes. Just don't answer the phone when someone is faxing you or you'll get an earful of fax tones.

Because PhoneFusion is a service, you can set the voicemail for all of your phone numbers (home, work) to forward to the same voicemail box, so you can consolidate all of your incoming voicemail messages in one place. Also, you should log into your account on the PhoneFusion Web site (www.phonefusion.com) to get access to a number of settings that you can't get to within the app.

Best features

The cool thing about all of this is that it's free! What is perhaps the *best* Visual VoiceMail feature sadly is not free — a transcription service that turns all of your voicemail messages into text you can read (see the figure on the right). When you first install Visual VoiceMail, you get this feature free for 30 days; if you want to keep using it beyond that, you have to pay for it. This service starts at a very reasonable $0.99 per month for automated transcriptions, and is well worth this small investment.

Worst features

Visual VoiceMail works great and I have no complaints about the app or the service. The only problem I encountered was that I sometimes mistakenly checked my phone's default voicemail using the voicemail app that came with the phone — instead of using the Visual VoiceMail app — and then couldn't understand why I didn't have any messages.

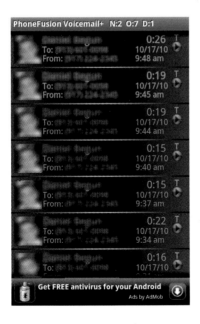

Handcent SMS
Free (ad supported)

Handcent SMS is messaging on steroids. It's meant to replace your phone's default messaging application (but it can also work in tandem with it). It fully supports SMS and MMS messages, and its customizable interface lets you change almost every aspect of how it looks. You can speak your messages and it will convert them to text; it can also speak messages you've received. You can send messages out to entire groups in one fell swoop, and add senders to a blacklist if you never want to hear from them again. You can create different notification settings for each contact from whom you receive messages. You can choose from a list of pre-canned messages, such as "I'm running late." You can add a signature to your messages and set outgoing messages to automatically split when they exceed 160 characters.

I've barely skimmed the surface, but my favorite feature is that Handcent SMS automatically pops up a window when you receive a message, regardless of what app you're using at the time. You can even reply to the message directly from this pop-up window.

I Am Here
Free

I don't know if it will ever catch on, but a PhD student in Australia by the name of Matthew Kwan created a standard called GeoSMS, which lets you send your precise coordinates (using a technique called "geotagging") via text messaging. The idea is that you can quickly tell someone *exactly* where you are just by texting him or her.

As a proof of concept, Kwan created the very simple I Am Here app, which grabs your current location and then passes it along to whatever messaging app your device uses. The recipient gets a message that includes your current latitude and longitude. If the recipient has an app that supports the GeoSMS standard, he can see where you are on a map or follow a compass needle that points him in your direction. Regretfully, as of when I wrote this, the *only* app that supports GeoSMS is I Am Here. But if you and the person you're texting with are both using it, you can easily find each other, even in large crowds.

Mr. Number Call Block
Free

March 10, 1876, is often considered when the very first phone call was made. What is not as well known is that March 11, 1876, is when the first telemarketing call was made. It's been downhill ever since. We all get calls we'd rather not receive, be it someone trying to sell us something or a long-lost friend whom we wish would stay lost. With Mr. Number Call Block (formerly Call Block Unlimited), you'll never be bothered again by unwanted callers or text messages.

To block specific callers or texters, you add them to the app's black-list by entering their phone numbers or choosing them from your phone's contacts. Add callers as exceptions to the blacklist to ensure that their calls make it through. You can block entire area codes, numbers that don't have Caller ID identifiers (also known as blocked or private numbers), callers who aren't in your contacts, or even block all "Suspected spam." Depending on the setting you choose, all blocked calls are either sent directly to voicemail or the phone answers the call only to immediately hang up on the caller.

 ## Tango Video Calls
Free

When it comes to free video calling apps, it doesn't get much simpler than Tango Video Calls. You can conduct video and voice calls with other Tango users over Wi-Fi, 3G, and 4G connections, and that's pretty much it — no other bells and whistles. It accesses your device's contacts and automatically tells you which of them are also registered Tango users. You can send e-mail and SMS invites to anyone in your device's contacts, asking your contacts to install Tango on their devices. There's also an iPhone version of Tango, so you've got a pretty big pool of potential users.

 ## TiKL – Touch to Talk (PTT)
Free (ad supported)

TiKL – Touch to Talk (PTT) turns your device into a very simple-to-use, push-to-talk walkie-talkie. Since your device's contacts show up in TiKL, just select a user — or multiple users — and press and hold the big Talk button in the middle of the screen to start speaking to other users over Wi-Fi, 3G, and 4G. TiKL can also use your Facebook contacts. The only caveats are that the people you're trying to talk to must also have TiKL installed and the app has to be running (there's also an iPhone version of TiKL). I only wish I had a friend named Elmo, so I could say to him, "TiKL me, Elmo!"

4 Education and Children's Apps

 Flash of Genius
$0.99 to $2.99 US

For many parents, one of the biggest challenges to sending a kid off to college or grad school is the tuition. For kids, one of the biggest hurdles is likely to be the standardized tests that so many schools' admissions departments require. It's no wonder, then, that test prep has become such a big business — and the plethora of test-prep Android apps attests to this. The Flash of Genius series is one of the more innovative sets of test-prep apps. There are $0.99 versions of the app for PSAT and SAT preparation, a $1.99 version for the GRE, and a $2.99 "Complete" version that combines the word libraries from all three apps.

Flash of Genius uses the age-old flashcard concept. On one side of a card is a study word, and on the other side are the definition, root, and an example of the word used in a sentence. The following figure shows the back of a flashcard from Flash of Genius: SAT Vocab.

The heart of Flash of Genius is its Study mode, where it displays a random flashcard from its library. If you know the meaning of the word, tap the check mark and another random card appears. If you aren't sure or don't know the meaning, tap the question mark and the card flips over to display more information about the word.

The back of every flashcard has an X and a check mark. If after reading the definition you realize that you know it, tap the check mark. If you aren't familiar with the definition, tap the X.

 On the surface, Flash of Genius is a simple flashcard-based vocabulary-learning app. But underneath are powerful mathematical algorithms that adjust to your learning style. Flash of Genius remembers which words you get wrong and stacks the deck (so to speak) so that those words appear more often. It also creates special lesson cards for when you know a word, but miss another word that shares the same root (such as "prologue" and "epilogue," which share the root "loc/log/loq").

Flash of Genius also includes a Quiz mode that displays random flashcards — although the cards it "randomly" picks are heavily influenced by the words you've missed. You can set the quiz length from ten cards to the entire deck. You can also view a list of all the words in the library and see a detailed list of word roots.

Best features

If you tap the study word on the front or backside of a flashcard, Flash of Genius speaks the proper pronunciation of the word. If you tap a word's definition on the back of a flashcard, Flash of Genius opens a Web page to the word's definition on `Wiktionary.org`.

Worst features

The PSAT, SAT, and GRE versions of Flash of Genius have a library of only about 400 words each — with some words shared between these different versions. The Complete version — which combines the words from all three apps — has a library of about 750 words. Many might consider a word library of this size too small for thorough test-prep vocabulary studying. For a more exhaustive vocabulary library, you might want to consider the $6.99 GRE Vocab Droid Pro app, which has about 6,000 words.

antecedent

n.   something happening or existing
     before something else

root(s): **ante**—before
         ced/cede/ceed—go/yield

When we got to the lecture hall, the students from the
antecedent class were still filing out.

Kids Numbers and Math
$2.99 US

Some kids love math, others would rather go to the dentist than have to do even basic arithmetic. But Kids Numbers and Math aims to change that by introducing children to numbers and simple math concepts at an early age, and to even make it fun.

Kids just beginning to learn their numbers should start with the appropriately named Learning Numbers module. Each screen displays a number while a clear voice says the number aloud. Tap the back or forward arrow to scroll through the numbers sequentially, or you can set them to appear in random order. You can choose to see numbers 1 through 10, 10 through 20, or 1 through 20.

As you can see in the figure, the Count module displays a random number of flowers and puts four possible answers at the bottom of the screen. Tap the correct answer and a voice congratulates you. Tap the incorrect answer and the voice encourages you. These verbal cues are standard in all modules that require you to pick the correct answer from a group of possible results.

With the Choose Max Number module, hot-air balloons that have numbers on them bob up and down. Tap the balloon that has the highest number to move to the next screen. If you tap the wrong balloon, it sinks to the bottom of the screen. You can set this module to display two, three, or four balloons. You can also set the range of numbers that appears on the balloons from between just 1 and 10, or as many as from 1 to 100. The Choose Min Number module works the same way, except you're supposed to tap the balloon with the lowest number.

When children start learning to add numbers together, the Addition module can offer some good practice. The two numbers that need to be added together are displayed along with a group of apples and a bunch of pears — you're supposed to add the apples and the pears together. The Subtraction module works similarly, except that you subtract the number of apples that have been eaten (just leaving apple cores) from the total number of apples. Each Subtraction screen appears with the satisfying sound of someone taking a bite of an apple.

The Advanced Exercises module is definitely geared toward kids who already have a strong grasp of basic arithmetic. In this module, you have to both add *and* subtract. Here you'll see problems like "$8 - 6 + 2 = ?$"

The last module, Find a Match, is one of the simplest. This basically is a matching game where you have to find the matching numbers that are hiding somewhere behind a bunch of clouds. When you match two numbers, the two clouds vanish in a flash of lightning and a clap of thunder.

Best features

Part of what makes Kids Numbers and Math fun is its cute graphics, which should appeal to preschool-age kids. With many of the modules, you can shake your device and the onscreen image will change. For instance, when you shake the device with the Choose Max Number module, the clouds in the sky behind the balloons float away; shake it again and a rainbow appears.

The only part of the app that actually speaks the numbers being displayed is the Learning Numbers module. But you can set Kids Numbers and Math to speak these numbers in one of eight languages, including Chinese, Spanish, and Russian. This could be a great way to introduce kids to a new language.

Worst features

It would be great if the entire app were multi-lingual, so even the spoken instructions, congratulatory comments, and encouragements were delivered in the selected language.

LOL Libs
$1.99 US

Kids love word games — especially silly word games — and it often doesn't get much sillier than Mad Libs. Mad Libs is a game where you insert words into intentionally blank spaces in a short story. The catch is, someone else asks you for the words, and you don't know what the story is until you supply all the words. The resulting stories can frequently be unexpectedly funny. And as you need to supply words from specific parts of speech (such as a noun or adjective), kids playing the game can even brush up on their grammar and vocabulary.

LOL Libs is an Android app version of Mad Libs. LOL Libs comes with 64 stories you can choose from. If you play the game a lot, you could quickly whiz through all 64 stories; but the great thing is that each story comes out differently each time you play it (unless you play LOL Libs so often that you manage to memorize all 64 stories). If you feel particularly creative, you can even create your own LOL Libs stories with the built-in story editor.

After you choose a story, you see a screen in which you need to enter a word, such as in the figure on the left. You are instructed as to what part of speech that word needs to be, and also shown a couple of word examples. After you type in a word and tap the Enter button, you are taken to the next word, and so on, until all of the needed words are entered. After all the words are populated, the finished story appears, such as the one in the figure on the right.

If you feel a particular story is especially amusing, you can tap the Send button to share it with your friends via e-mail or SMS. You can also tap the Save button so that you can enjoy the story again. You can even hear it read aloud by tapping the Speak button — stories are read by Android's built-in text-to-speech feature. As Android's speech synthesis is rather emotionless and is known to sometimes mispronounce words, hearing your Android device read the story can sometimes add an additional layer of hilarity.

 Every time you enter a word into LOL Libs, that word gets saved to LOL Lib's Word Libraries. After enough words are entered, you can go into the Options and turn on Random mode. Now whenever you choose a story, the words for that story will be randomly populated from the libraries. If LOL Libs looks for a type of word that isn't in its libraries, it prompts you to enter the additional words it needs to complete the story. If the same words pop up too often when using Random mode, turn it off for a while so that you can further build up the libraries. You can also clear the contents of the Word Libraries if you want to start over, or perhaps you need to get rid of the evidence of a few vulgar words that someone else snuck in (surely, *you* didn't do it!).

Best features

Mad Libs is traditionally played with paper and pen and requires at least two players if you don't want to see the story while you're entering the words. While LOL Libs is certainly more enjoyable to play with a group, you can still easily play the game by yourself, since you won't see the story until after all the words are entered.

Worst features

Avid players will whiz through all 64 stories in no time; it would be great if there were more stories.

 **Math Workout Pro**
£0.64

Even our brains require some exercise from time to time, and Math Workout Pro purports to give your noodle some mental calisthenics. But although it is marketed primarily as a brain-exercise app, Math Workout Pro can also help kids who are trying to learn basic arithmetic, such as addition, subtraction, multiplication, and division.

Math Workout Pro includes eight different math "games" you can play (see the image on the left). Children just getting their math feet wet should probably stick to either the Addition & Subtraction or Multiplication & Division module, depending on their current learning level.

After you start a game, Math Workout Pro counts down from three, and then gives you your first question. In Easy mode, you see fairly basic questions, such as "5 + 6" or "10 ÷ 5." Type your answer using the onscreen keyboard, such as the one in the image on the right. At the end of the workout, your score is displayed, which is how long it took you to answer all of the questions plus a 5-second penalty for every wrong answer.

In the app's Options, you can set each game to last for 10, 20, or 50 questions. You can also set the difficulty to Easy, Medium, or Hard. In order to play any of the games in either the Medium or Hard mode, however, you first have to unlock these modes by answering a certain number of questions within a specific amount of time in the I'm Feeling Clever! game. I'm Feeling Clever! dishes out questions from both the Addition & Subtraction and Multiplication & Division modes. (I'm not sure what this says about me, but I'm still struggling to just unlock the Medium difficulty mode!)

If you're feeling particularly sharp-witted, you can take a stab at The Brain Cruncher game, which gives you a multistep math question. Each step displays for only a few seconds before the next part of the question replaces it. You might get a question that asks, "Start with 4, add 3, multiply by 2, divide by 7, multiply by 2, multiply by 3, divide by 12, add 10, multiply by 2, multiply by 2, and subtract 14." (In case you're wondering, the answer is 30.) You can choose between Low, Medium, and High Pressure settings, but you have to successfully complete each level a certain number of times before the next level is unlocked.

If you're feeling downright cocky, take the Online World Challenge. You must correctly answer 50 questions, and they get increasingly difficult as the game progresses. At the end, your score is measured against those of other users who also took the challenge that day. If you're anything like me, prepare to be humiliated.

For a little more fun, try your luck with the Math Blaster Challenge. It is sort of like a math version of Space Invaders. Math questions float down the screen in bubbles; you have to "zap" them with the correct answer before they reach the bottom of the screen.

The final game, Mental Math Master, adds a few extra levels of difficulty: It only speaks the math questions and doesn't let you see them, and it asks harder questions than you find in the other modules.

Best features

The Times Table Practice module lets you choose which times tables you want to review, up to 15; you also can run the tables sequentially or randomly.

Worst features

I originally grumbled that the app was too expensive; but that's when it cost £2.95. Now at £0.64 (which is about $1.00 US), I can't complain. If that's still too rich for you and you don't mind seeing ads while you cogitate on math problems, try Math Workout — the free version of this app.

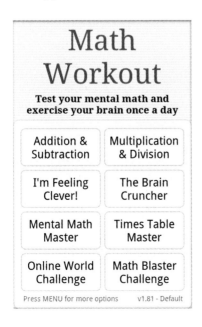

Preschool Learning
$1.99 US

Preschool Learning is really four apps in one. It includes a set of virtual alphabet blocks, a coloring book, letter tracing, and a matching game. The four activities combined can certainly keep a preschool-age kid occupied for a little while — perhaps during a long ride in the car. And to assuage any possible guilt you might feel from letting your child "play games" on your Android device, remember that the activities actually have educational value.

The Alphabet Blocks activity includes 26 realistic-looking three-dimensional blocks you can spin and rotate to see any of their six sides. Two sides of each block display a letter, while the other four sides show objects that start with that letter. For instance, the "S" block includes images of the sun, a star, a sheep, and a snake. Perhaps the only thing missing here is the capability to stack the blocks and then knock them over — one of my daughter's favorite pastimes.

The Colors and Textures activity includes a bunch of line drawings of things like teddy bears, puppies, and kittens. You can fill the spaces between the lines with a wide range of colors or textures, freehand draw anywhere on the page, and stick scrapbook art images wherever your heart desires. You can undo up to your last three additions to the page and even save your masterpiece. If you get tired of coloring the pages, you can load virtually any image stored on your device and bedazzle it until it's unrecognizable.

With Letter Tracing, choose from uppercase letters, lowercase letters, or numbers. A voice speaks the displayed letter or number, and arrows point in the direction to trace the letter or number. If that isn't enough, a train or caterpillar also moves along the letter or number in the direction that it should be traced. You can see the letter "S" being traced in the figure on the left.

Match Party is a simple matching game that's made up of 30 cards, of which you can turn over any two cards at a time. This is primarily a memory game, where you try to remember where you previously saw an image.

Depending on the age of your child and how much experience your child has using your device, you might need to supervise or provide some guidance along the way. Then again, if your child is anything like my three-year-old daughter, she probably knows how to use your device better than you do.

Best features

You might be horrified at the prospect of putting your precious and expensive device in the hands of your child. Preschool Learning can't do much to avoid peanut-butter smudges or prevent a case of the dropsies, but it can deter your child from making phone calls or opening other apps. Preschool Learning includes a "child lock" feature, which when engaged, disables most of the controls on your device. Your device's Menu button is still functional; but if your kid taps it — sending the display back to the main Android home screen — an alarm sounds, alerting you that your child has exited the app. The little red padlock in the lower-left corner of the figure on the right shows that the child lock is engaged.

Worst features

The Colors and Textures module is a bit awkward to use. It has only one zoom level, and it's too easy to accidentally fill in spaces with colors when you don't mean to.

Five Pumpkins
Free

Five Pumpkins is not an Android app, but is actually the name of the company that makes a bunch of great educational flashcard apps for preschool-age kids. For learning letters and words: ABCs teaches the alphabet; Sight Words teaches short two- to four-letter words, like "up," "car," and "look" (both of these apps can display cards in upper- and lowercase). For learning numbers: Numbers teaches 0 through 10; Numbers 50 teaches 1 through 50.The Colors, Shapes, and Days/Months apps teach exactly what their names imply. Finally, On the Go teaches the names of vehicles, such as bicycle, fire engine, and helicopter.

A clear-sounding female voice pronounces what's on the card (some apps even have image and word examples of the letters, numbers, or colors on the backside of the cards). You can also turn on Quiz mode. It won't speak the card name until you tap the screen. Most of the apps also include a Favorites mode. It displays only those cards that you've starred. Best of all, all of these apps are cost- and ad-free!

LangLearner SpellingBee
Free

LangLearner SpellingBee lets you brush up on your spelling using a format that's similar to what you might experience at a real spelling bee — minus the fellow contestants and overanxious parents. First, pick the level of the words you'll be quizzed on. They range from Kindergarten up to eighth-grade level words, or even winning words from actual spelling bees. The quiz begins with a clearly pronounced word. You can either tap the Spell It! button and speak what you think is the proper spelling of the word, or tap the Type It! button and spell the word using your device's keyboard. The screen displays either "Wrong, try again" or "CORRECT!" — depending on whether you spelled the word correctly. You can't ask for a definition, origin, or usage in a sentence, however; for that you'll need to enter a real spelling bee.

The Rescue of Ginger
$0.99 US

The Rescue of Ginger, an interactive storybook, follows the adventures of Madera Monkey and Figaro Frog, who — in their superhero identities as Carbon Girl and Adhero — try to find Mrs. Applebottom's missing cat, Ginger. Every page features cute hand-drawn art, animations, and numerous elements that you can interact with; six of the pages include activities based on size, color, or shape recognition. If The Rescue of Ginger is a hit with your kids, check out the sequel, Save The Day ($0.99 in the Android Market).

 # TechMind Animal Sounds
Free

So many animal sounds apps are available for Android devices that I wonder just how hard it can really be to program an audio clip of oinking to play whenever you tap an image of a pig. (Sure to confuse you, many of these are simply called "Animal Sounds.") TechMind Animal Sounds rises above the din, however, with a couple of cool features that other apps lack.

Recognizing that some animals can frighten young kids, the app includes the option of hiding the image and sound of some of the scarier animals, like the bear and the wolf. But also recognizing that some older kids might want to learn more about the animals, TechMind Animal Sounds has an option that launches Wikipedia when you tap the name of an animal. After listening to the very odd-sounding calls of a peacock, I followed the link to Wikipedia and learned that a baby peacock is called a peachick.

 # Toddler Lock
Free (ad supported)

Toddler Lock is a simple drawing app for preschoolers. Drag your finger around the screen to draw neon-colored lines or tap the display to place multicolored shapes. Every time you touch the screen, the app plays music that sounds like wind chimes. Toddler Lock gets it name from the fact that it "locks" your Android device so that no matter which buttons your youngsters start mashing, they won't be able to access anything else on your device.

 To exit the app, tap the four corners of the screen in a clockwise manner. If your device has a physical keyboard, you can press the Q key, P key, and then the spacebar.

5 Entertainment

Doodledroid
$0.99 US

With so much art being created electronically these days, it makes sense that the practice should extend to Android devices. You might think that it would be too difficult to produce anything that looks halfway decent on the small screen of an Android phone, but you'd be surprised. Don't take my word for it — look at the drawings on www.doodledroid.net, all of which were created with Doodledroid, a surprisingly robust drawing program.

Start with a blank canvas, open an existing image, or import a photo to which you can add your touches. When you import a photo, Doodledroid forces you to choose just a portion of the photo that will fit in its portrait-mode screen.

If you're working with a blank canvas, the best place to start is to pick the background color for the canvas. You can set the background color several ways. The figure on the left shows the Spectrum Selector tab, where you set the saturation slider on the bottom, and then drag your finger across the color spectrum in the middle of the screen until you find the color you want. If you want to fine-tune the color, select the Color Adjust tab, which includes sliders for hue, saturation, and value. If an image is already on the canvas, you can select the Color Picker tab, which lets you select a color from the image.

Next, select the drawing tool you want to use. Choose from Brush, Eraser, Fill, and Smudge. Then go into the Adjust menu to access the settings for the tool. The settings are basic for all of the tools, except for Brush, which you can see in the figure on the right.

Choose from 21 Brush Patterns, and set the brush's Tip Width, Base Width, and Transparency. Tip Width is the width when the brush moves in a straight line; Base Width is the brush's width when it turns. A Dynamic setting makes the brush strokes transparent when you move the brush quickly across the canvas. A preview window shows an example of what the brush stroke will look like based on the current settings. Setting the color for the Brush (or Fill tool) uses the same color options as the Background color.

If you make a mistake, Doodledroid can undo your last five edits. Undo by pressing your device's Volume Up button, and redo by pressing the Volume Down button. You can also zoom in 2x or 4x by pressing your device's trackball or tapping the screen with two fingers. While zoomed in, you can pan around the drawing using the trackball or the small Zoom windows that appears in the lower-right corner.

Best features

You don't have to worry about forgetting to save your work. When you exit Doodledroid, your image is automatically saved. So even if you accidentally hit your device's Home button or the Back button one too many times, your masterpiece is safe, which is very comforting, except that . . .

Worst features

. . . the image gets flattened to a single layer when you quit out of Doodledroid. This means you can't undo any of the last five changes or change the background color.

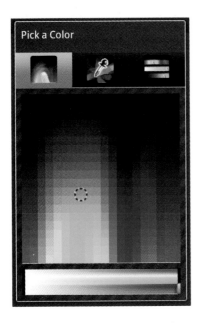
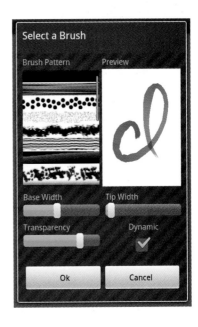

Gigbox
Free

If you're a fan of popular music and you like going to see bands play live, then Gigbox will quickly become your best friend. Gigbox keeps track of your favorite performers and lets you know when they have a gig coming up, and whether that show is happening nearby.

If you are a frequent user of the Last.fm Internet radio streaming site (www.last.fm), Gigbox can connect with your Last.fm account to get an instant look at your favorite artists. This saves you tons of time, because otherwise you must manually enter all of the performers you want to track.

The primary section of Gigbox is the Watchlist. This is the section you populate with performers you want to track. You can add artists to the Watchlist several ways. One way is to choose them from the top 50 performers from your Last.fm account. You can also just type in the artists' names and search for them. My favorite way to add artists to the Watchlist is to let Gigbox search the device's SD card for all music files that are installed, and it figures out who the performers are for most of the songs.

After the Watchlist is populated with your favorite artists, tap the Sync Now button and Gigbox connects to the Internet and searches for any scheduled live shows. The figure on the left shows that Lady Gaga has 66 scheduled gigs, two of which are nearby. In Gigbox's setting, you set "nearby" to be between 10 and 250 miles from your location — Gigbox uses your device's GPS location services to determine your location.

Tap an artist's name and a list of all known upcoming gigs appears. You can sort the list by date, distance (closer gigs appear higher in the list), or by placing all the new gigs since the last time you synced at the top of the list.

Tap an event and choose from options such as I'm Attending This Event, Add to Calendar, and Tweet This Event. You can also call up the venue's location on a map and even get directions. If you don't already have tickets, Gigbox includes links to some shows at the Bandsintown and TicketMaster online ticket-buying services.

Gigbox also include a Search feature where you can look for information on artists who aren't in your Watchlist. If you get a sudden hankering to head out and see some live music right now, you can also search for gigs based on location or venue. The figure on the right displays the shows scheduled to play at the Beacon Theater in New York City when I did my search.

When you search for an artist or select an artist from a list, you can see all the events that the performer is scheduled for, see photos and YouTube videos, and get more info about the artist. The info screen includes a biography of the performer and a list of similar artists.

Gigbox users who bring their Android devices with them to live shows can use the Gigbox Live feature to chat with other concert goers, rate the show, and even upload photos.

Best features

Gigbox keeps you up to date on where your favorite artists are performing and also lets you explore new artists you might not be familiar with.

Worst features

Gigbox focuses primarily on popular artists. You aren't likely to find concerts listed for many less mainstream performers, local artists, or performers from less commercial musical genres, like jazz or blues.

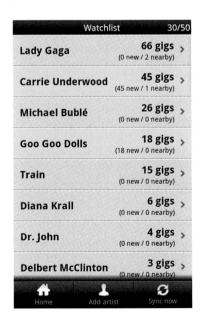

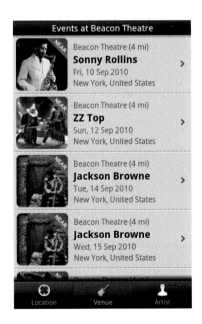

Movies by Flixster
Free

If you are a true movie buff, then you really can't do without Movies by Flixster. It keeps you in the know about upcoming film and DVD releases, and you can also watch trailers, purchase tickets, and even access your Netflix queue.

The Box Office tab, which you can see in the figure on the left, lists entries for the films that are opening this week, current box-office leaders, and other films that are currently playing in theaters. Each movie listing shows a thumbnail of the movie poster, who stars in it, its film rating, its running time, and how much the movie has grossed so far. The listings also include Tomatometer ratings from the film-review site, Rotten Tomatoes (www.rottentomatoes.com). A score of at least 60 percent earns a fresh tomato, while a score below 60 percent gets a rotten tomato.

When you tap on a listing, a page with information about that movie appears, such the one for the film, *Tangled,* in the figure on the right. You can watch the movie's trailer, see showtimes for local theaters, and view promotional photos. If you have a free Flixster (www.flixster.com) account, you can assign your own five-star rating to a movie, write a review, or state that you want to see it — all of which is shared with other Flixster users.

Scroll down the screen and you see a synopsis of the film, as well as entries for its director and cast members. You can select these entries to see short biographies, photos, and complete filmographies.

Below that are reviews from professional movie critics. Select any of these entries to read the entire review on the site where it originally appeared. Below that are reviews from Flixster users.

The Upcoming tab is meant primarily for watching trailers for movies that aren't out yet. It works similar to the Box Office tab, except that no showtimes appear.

When you tap the Theaters tab, it displays theaters that are close by. You can also search for theaters by name or see them on a map. You can tap on the theater's address and Google Maps opens, from which you can get driving directions to the theater. For some theaters, you can even purchase tickets using a credit card.

The DVD tab provides similar information to that on the Box Office tab, except that the entries here pertain to DVDs that have just come out or will soon be released. You can also browse older DVDs by categories, such as comedy, documentary, or romance.

Press your device's Menu button to access Movies by Flixster's Search feature, which provides info about nearly *any* movie, old or new. I wanted to test just how exhaustive the search was, so I looked for the 1925 Charlie Chaplin movie, *The Gold Rush*. Movies by Flixster found it and provided lots of details.

The last tab is labeled My Movies, and it includes entries for the movies you rated and those you marked that you wanted to see. You can also see entries for the users you "friended" on Flixster and view their recent ratings and reviews.

Best features

If you have a Netflix account, you can use Movies by Flixster to reorder or remove movies from your DVD and Watch Instantly queues. Even better, a Save to Netflix Queue button appears with most movie listings (see the figure on the right). You can add DVDs to the top or bottom of your queue, or save them to your queue if they haven't been released yet.

Worst features

Flixster.com is also a social networking site for like-minded film fans. Although you can see what your friends are up to with the Movies by Flixster app, you can't actually add new friends with the app — that can only be done on the Flixster Web site. Flixster can, however, integrate with Facebook, instantly connecting you with all your Facebook friends.

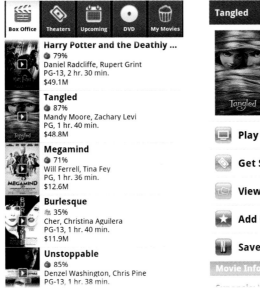

PicSay Pro Photo Editor
€2.99

With PicSay Pro's wealth of photo manipulation features, I could easily include it in the Photography and Video chapter instead of here in the Entertainment chapter. But PicSay Pro includes so many entertaining features that you'll probably spend more time adding funny word balloons and clip-art stickers to photos than adjusting image exposure or color temperature.

In the figure on the left, I had some fun with a picture of my daughter scrambling up a climbing wall. The first thing I did was add a Word Balloon. I typed in the text I wanted to appear in the balloon, selected the balloon style and color pattern, font and text size, and then fine-tuned the text, fill, and outline colors (with options for setting the hue, saturation, and brightness).

With the balloon placed on the image, I adjusted the horizontal and vertical dimensions of it using a simple and intuitive tool that allows me stretch and squish the balloon just by dragging the tool around the screen. Next, I dragged the balloon to where I wanted it to sit. Finally, I tapped the balloon's "tail" and dragged it to where I wanted it to sit — this automatically stretches or shrinks the tail, relative to where it connects with the balloon.

I chose not to put a Title on the image, but if I had, there are many different fonts and color styles to choose from. There are also fine-tune color controls for the title's text and outline colors. You can also reposition a title and control its horizontal and vertical dimensions.

Next came the Stickers, with which I had the most fun. You can see just some of the available sticker categories in the figure on the right. The angel wings came from the Accessories section, the halo from Hats & Helmets, the teddy bear from Romance, and the butterfly from Nature. I placed the stickers on the image, and then resized and rotated them until I was happy with how they looked.

 If you tap an element on the page, a pop-up menu gives you additional editing options. For any item, you can edit Effects (such as contrast and brightness), Arrange which elements will sit above overlapping items, and even Delete an element. Tiles and Stickers have a Transform option, which lets you Flip the item, Rotate it, or Reset it back to its default settings, and a Perspective Tool that lets you stretch or squish the item from any of the four corners of a bounding box.

I'm almost out of space here, and I've barely scratched the surface of what PicSay Pro can do. You can apply a ton of Effects to any underlying photo, such as adjusting the tint or sharpness; distortions, such as twirl or stretch; artistic embellishments, such as pencil sketch or neon; photo effects, such as sepia toning or soft glow; and filters, such as vignette or spotlight.

When you are satisfied with the end result, you can save the image to your device's SD card, turn it into your device's wallpaper, e-mail it, or share it with any number of social networking services.

Best features

It's impossible to pick any one feature that stands out above any others — everything here is great!

Worst features

The one thing sorely missing from PicSay Pro is a global undo feature that lets you undo your last several edits.

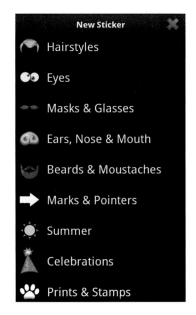

TV.com
Free (ad supported)

Watching video-on-demand on a handheld mobile device is often considered the holy grail of mobile media consumption. I'm not talking about cute videos of cats flushing toilets on YouTube, but watching full-length movies and TV shows.

As of when I wrote this, only one Android app delivered this experience, the Blockbuster On Demand app. The trouble is, only owners of a small handful of phones available through T-Mobile and Verizon can access the app. If you have any other Android device, you're out of luck.

By the time you read this, however, the Blockbuster app might be available for more devices. Also, when I wrote this, rumors of other video-on-demand services for Android devices were brewing. Netflix for Android, anyone? For all I know, right now you could be sitting in a flying car, being driven by a robot driver, while watching the President of the World give her inauguration speech. (Thus are the perils of working in the archaic medium of print, where there is such a long lead time.)

My prognosticating aside, there's already an app that delivers at least some full-length TV episodes on demand — TV.com — and it's available for any Android device that can install apps from the Android Market. TV.com is the Android app version of the Web site of the same name, which CBS Entertainment owns; therefore, much of the available content in the TV.com app is from CBS-owned sources.

You find full-length episodes from a number of popular CBS shows, such as *CSI: Miami, 60 Minutes,* and *Big Brother* (see the figure on the left). Watch all of these shows streamed over a Wi-Fi connection. If your device has a data plan (as most Android phones do), you can watch many of TV.com's episodes via the data connection as well, but some episodes are available for streaming only via Wi-Fi. No matter how you watch a full episode, though, be prepared to sit through a few commercials.

In addition to full episodes, hundreds of short clips are also available for nearly every show that airs on CBS. The video clips go way beyond just what airs on CBS itself, however. You find clips from other CBS-owned sources as well, such as The CW Television Network, Showtime, and CNET.

If there are particular shows that you watch, you can add them to the My TV section, where you can see all the available clips and full episodes for your shows. Also note that the available content constantly changes, so don't be surprised if a full episode that is available one week is nowhere to be seen a week later.

If all you're interested in doing is seeing which full episodes are available for watching, press your device's Menu button and then tap the Shows button. This takes you to the Full Episodes page. When I recently visited this page, 29 different TV shows had at least some full episodes available for viewing; however, they weren't all current TV shows.

Best features

By far, my favorite feature of TV.com is the Classic TV section. Here you find episodes from a number of TV shows from the days of yore. I can easily live without episodes of *Dynasty* and *Melrose Place,* but I'm more than a little giddy that I can watch full episodes from *The Twilight Zone* and the original *Star Trek* series. The figure on the right shows some of the available classic TV episodes.

Worst features

Isn't it obvious what TV.com's worst feature is? It needs more full-length episodes! I want more than just 31 episodes of *Star Trek!*

Backgrounds
Free (ad supported)

Backgrounds is a boon for Android device users and photographers. When I wrote this, there were more than 13,000 free images available that Backgrounds users could install as their wallpaper or contacts icons. These images come from a growing pool of photographs and illustrations that artists upload to the Backgrounds app flickr (www. flickr.com) group. This gets potentially many more people looking at artists' creations; Backgrounds' developer claims that the app has been downloaded nearly 25 million times (this includes the iPhone and Palm Pre versions of Background as well).

Search for images, or pick them from the Popular or Recent tabs, which show you what other folks have recently downloaded to their devices. You can also choose images from a long list of Categories, such as Food, Sunsets, and Travel. Many of these are high-quality images created by professional photographers.

If your personal philosophy is that variety is the spice of life, then you can set Backgrounds to randomly change your device's background image hourly, every 12 hours, or once per day, from those images you flag as favorites.

E! Online
Free (ad supported)

If you're fixated on the lives of the rich and famous, there's a good chance that your TV is often tuned to the E! channel. But how do you keep up with the latest celebrity gossip when you're on the go?

With the E! Online app, that's how. You can read about the Hollywood elite's latest shenanigans and also watch featured clips from E! shows, such as *Keeping Up with the Kardashians* and *The Soup*. In fact, a number of E!'s more popular shows offer a veritable smorgasbord of video clips to watch.

There's even a separate "Top Celebs" section, where you can scroll through a long list of A-list celebrities. Tap an entry to read news stories and watch videos about that particular person. You can even create your own customized list of celebrities to follow.

Mabilo Ringtones
Free (ad supported)

If you are the type to change your phone's ringtone more frequently than you change your underwear — or assign a different ringtone to every contact in your address book — then Mabilo Ringtones is for you. Mabilo Ringtones lets you browse, search, preview, and download ringtones from a library of more than a 200,000 user-uploaded MP3s.

You might not have much luck if you're looking for a song that isn't very popular. Also, the recording quality of some of the ringtones leaves a bit to be desired. But with persistence, you will find the perfect ringtone to assign to Aunt Gladys.

Many of these ringtones were created by users who don't have the legal rights to the songs. That means neither do you.

Onion News Network
Free (ad supported)

When you're in the mood for a good belly laugh, fire up Onion News Network and watch any of its satiric and often irreverent news videos. If you aren't familiar with the Onion News Network (also known as ONN), it is an offshoot of the news parody Web site, The Onion (www.theonion.com).

ONN news videos look an awful lot like the real thing, including real-looking news anchors and correspondents, actual news sets, slick infographics, and all of the other trappings that we expect from legitimate news sources. You might even momentarily forget what you're watching is fake, until someone says something so incredulous that it can't possibly be true . . . or can it?

TV Guide Mobile
Free (ad supported)

Want to know what's on TV tonight or up to a week from now? Just launch TV Guide Mobile, and it gives you the entire lineup for your local provider's or over-the-air channels. You can set channels as favorites so you can quickly see what's showing on just those channels right now. You can also set shows as favorites, which shows you the next time those shows will air. And while you have TV Guide Mobile running, you might as well as take a peek at the News section to catch up the latest TV-related news.

6 Finance

Balance Book – Profit Tracker
$4.99 US

Did you know that approximately 99.7 percent of the businesses in the U.S. are considered small businesses? That's about 27.5 million businesses, of which roughly 14.3 million are run from people's homes. Many of these are sole proprietorships, which means that methods for tracking sales and expenses vary from using high-end accounting software to notes scribbled onto napkins with crayons.

If your small business's accounting needs are fairly simple and you're the type to have your Android device never more than an arm's reach away from you, Balance Book – Profit Tracker might just make your life a whole lot easier. With just a few quick taps, you can enter all of your business's expenses and sales.

Do this by selecting the Costs and Sales module (see the figure on the left) from the app's home screen. From there you select either the Costs and Expenses tab or the Sales tab. For costs and expenses, pick from a list of existing categories, or create a new category. Then enter the cost of the item (Balance Book – Profit Tracker supports currencies from 26 countries), the date and time of the purchase, and any relevant comments (such as "check with accountant to confirm sunscreen is a legitimate business expense").

Entering sales (for products, goods, or services) works similarly in that you choose a category or create a new one. You then enter the unit price, quantity, and date and time of the sale. That's all that's required, but there are also fields where you can enter any processing-cost rates you incur (such as commissions), any additional costs (such as shipping), and comments (such as "loyal customer, next time give him a complimentary whoopee cushion").

After you enter some sales and expenses, you can view the entries in the Balance Sheet module (see the figure on the right). You can view all entered data, just expenses, income, or specific categories. You can view the balance sheet by day, week, or month. If you tap and hold an entry, you can edit it, delete it, or launch your device's camera to take a snapshot of the item's receipt.

Balance Book – Profit Tracker also includes a Charts and Diagrams module that displays a bar graph and a line chart of your expenses versus your income. This module can view the same data sets that the Balance Sheet does, except that Charts and Diagrams doesn't show data for an individual day — just for a week or month at a time.

The Business Tools module includes a simple calculator, a price and revenue calculator, and a loan calculator. If you are fan of redundancy, you can manually make a backup of the database or set Balance Book – Profit Tracker to automatically create a backup whenever you exit the app. You can also restore your data from a backed up database file.

Best features

You can export your data to a CSV file, which you can then send as an e-mail attachment.

Worst features

You can't assign default prices to items you enter on the sales screen. This means that you must re-enter the price every time for a sale, no matter how frequently you sell that specific item.

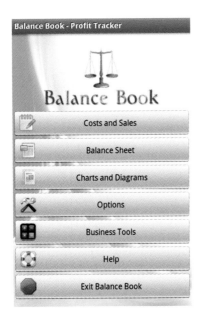

Bloomberg

Free (ad supported)

It's been said that a wise investor is an informed investor. And if you rely on Bloomberg LP for your financial information, you'd be hard-pressed to be any *more* financially informed. Bloomberg LP professes that it is "the most trusted source of financial information." Although I doubt there is any way to unequivocally prove this, you have to give at least some credit to a company that was founded by a man who became a multibillionaire and Mayor of New York City.

There are any number of ways to get your fill of financial fortitude from Bloomberg LP, including from TV, radio, the Internet, and now from the Bloomberg Android app. The Bloomberg app divvies up the wisdom it disseminates into four sections: News, Markets, My Stocks, and Stock Finder.

When you first launch Bloomberg, its News page delivers stories that fall into the Worldwide category and stories that are Exclusive to Bloomberg. If you tap the Edit button on the upper-right corner of the screen (see the figure on the left), you can add from a plethora of additional categories to the list of news stories displayed. Available categories include varied topics like Emerging Markets, Health Care, China, and even U.S. Sports.

Don't go crazy and add every category under the sun. The more categories you add, the longer it takes Bloomberg to download all those news stories to your device.

The Markets section includes basic data on major Equity Indices, Commodities, Bonds, and Currencies. Of these, only the Equity Indices include additional information, such as an index's open, high, low, and price-earnings ratio. Each index also includes a 52-week summary chart that you can tap to expand to fill the screen in landscape mode. In this mode, you can view the index's one-day, one-month, six-month, one-year, and five-year charts. Most indexes also include an Industry Movers section broken out by chart and table. You also find a Stock Movers section that identifies the Leaders and Laggers.

The My Stocks screen is where you enter your own portfolio's holdings or those stocks you wish to follow. You can just enter the stock symbol to see the daily percent change, or can also input the number of shares you own and the price per share you paid for them, in order to track the stock's value. Note that you don't have to know the specific stock symbol; you can just enter the company's name and Bloomberg displays a list of matching company stocks to choose from.

If you just want to find out information about a specific company, use the Stock Finder section to search for it. After you find the listing for the company you are looking for, tap it to see a screen full of detailed information that looks similar to what the index screens look like. The figure on the right shows the stock information screen for Google.

Best features

When it comes to financial information to help you make informed investment decisions, Bloomberg can't be beat with the depth and breadth of information it provides.

Worst features

Some readers of the Bloomberg Web site (www.bloomberg.com) use the site to track their portfolios. Unfortunately, the Bloomberg app cannot sync with this data; if you want to see your portfolio on the site and in the app, you must input all your information twice.

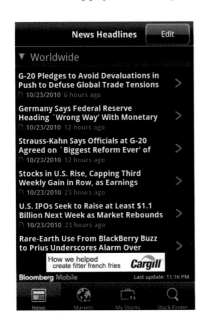

Debt Payoff Planner
$0.99 US

For people with multiple credit cards with large balances, just thinking about how to pay off all that debt can feel overwhelming. And let's not forget about student loans, auto loans, and mortgages.

For the low, low price of $0.99, Debt Payoff Planner can steer you in the right direction and show you what you need to do to become debt free. First, you need to provide details about all of your debts. For each debt, enter the creditor's name, current balance, interest rate, and the date that the payment is due each month. If the debt has a promotional interest rate, enter that special rate and how many more months until the rate skyrockets.

Next, enter the total amount of money you plan on putting toward all your debts each month. Debt Payoff Planner lets you choose from five strategies for paying off your debt:

- ✔ Highest Interest First
- ✔ Lowest Balance First
- ✔ Minimum Payment Only
- ✔ As Keyed-In Order
- ✔ Highest Balance First

After you pick a strategy, tap the Calculate button (see the figure on the left). An Amortization screen appears and shows you how much money you should pay toward each of your debts every month. As you can see in the figure on the right, the top of this screen also shows you when you'll be debt free and the total interest you'll have paid. This is assuming, of course, that you don't add any new debt onto your existing debt. If you do, you can make any necessary changes to the debt details — but don't feign surprise when that debt-free date keeps slipping away from you

 Scroll down the Amortization screen to see how the payment schedule changes over time after you pay off some of the individual debts. Also, depending on the size of your device's screen, not all of your debts may appear. In my case, to see the BofA debt (from the figure on the left), I either had to scroll to the right of the screen or turn my device on its side to switch the view to landscape mode.

If you want, you can choose to view your debt amortization displayed as a line chart. There's something very satisfying about seeing the lines that represent your debts disappear into nothingness. You might want to gloss over the pie chart, however, that shows how much of what you're paying is principal and how much is interest — it'll just depress you. You can also tap any of the Due By buttons on the Amortization screen to get a detailed look at the current balance, total payments made, total principal paid, and total interest paid to date for each account.

Best features

Debt Payoff Planner takes the guessing out of how to get out of debt and helps you formulate a solid plan to become debt free.

Worst features

The interface can be a bit confusing — especially for those who might not be familiar with all the terms the apps uses (like amortization). That said, a detailed help page explains most of this and even provides a few examples.

Debt Payoff Planner :: Amortization			
Tip: Click on the Date to get More details			
Payment Per Term:			500.00
Choosen Strategy: **Highest Interest First**			
Debt Free By:			**Jun 2013**
Total Interest:			**1150.85**
Due By	**HSBC**	**Citibank**	**Chase**
Jul 2011	72.24	79.74	121.75
Aug 2011	72.24	79.74	121.75
Sep 2011	72.24	79.74	121.75
Oct 2011	72.24	79.74	121.75
Nov 2011	21.45	130.53	121.75
Dec 2011	-	151.98	121.75
Jan 2012	-	151.98	121.75
Feb 2012	-	151.98	121.75

EasyMoney
$9.95 US

Contrary to what this app's name implies, EasyMoney is not about get-rich-quick schemes. What it *is* about is easily managing your bank accounts, credit cards, and bills. Think of EasyMoney as a check register on steroids. You can track your income and daily expenses for multiple accounts, and also create monthly budgets, set up bill reminders, and even generate reports to see where your money is going.

First, you must create account entries for each of the accounts you want to track, such as checking, savings, and credit cards. Give the account a name, description, and starting balance, and set what currency to use (choose from 107 currencies, and you even use different currencies for your different accounts, such as your secret offshore account in the Cayman Islands). You can also set a monthly budget for each account and exclude the account from the total balance of all of your accounts. All accounts appear on the Accounts Overview page.

Select an account to see the transactions you previously entered or to add new transactions. When you add transactions, you supply the payee or income source, the amount, the date and specify it is a withdrawal or deposit. You can also add a note (such as a check number) and assign it to a category, which comes in handy when you want to analyze your spending or keep to a budget. You can always edit transactions, such as updating their status to cleared, uncleared, reconciled, or void.

EasyMoney comes with a number of preset categories, but you can add as many custom categories as you want. You can give each category a name, set whether it's income or an expense, give it a description, and even assign a color to it — these colors appear in the register and are also used when you generate reports.

You don't have to shell out ten bucks to find out if EasyMoney is right for you. You can install a free, trial version that is fully functional for 30 days. If you like it, you can upgrade to the paid version from within the app.

Best features

EasyMoney has three standout features: budgets, reports, and bill reminders.

- ✔ **Budgets:** Create a budget item for each category you want to track, and they all appear on a Monthly Budget screen that shows if you are under or over budget. In the figure on the left, you can see I already spent more on Android apps than I had budgeted for.

- ✔ **Reports:** Generate reports for a variety of income and expense categories for different accounts and time periods. The figure on the right is an example of the Expenses by Category report.

- ✔ **Bill reminders:** When you set bill reminders, you supply the payee and the estimated amount, assign it a category, put in the due date, and set whether it repeats — and if so, how frequently. You can also choose how many days before a bill is due for EasyMoney to send a reminder, which appears as a notification in your device's status bar.

Worst features

When you enter transactions, you have the options to state if they repeat and how often they occur. You'd think that this would automatically create a bill reminder entry, but it doesn't. The only way to create a bill reminder is to enter it manually.

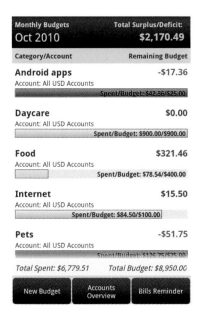

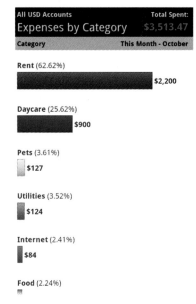

Pageonce – Money & Bills

Free (ad supported)

Pageonce – Money & Bills is a financial manager that helps keep track of your bank account balances, credit card charges, and investments by gathering data from your online accounts. Above and beyond that, it also keeps you up to date on all sorts of online shopping, utility (as in your home's gas, electric, and water service), frequent flyer, and even social networking accounts you have. I like to think of Pageonce – Money & Bills as a dashboard that gives a quick overview of your online footprint—no matter how big your feet might be.

I'm amazed at the vast number of financial institutions that Pageonce – Money & Bills has access to. Chances are your bank, credit card company, or investment house is one of the many companies from which Pageonce – Money & Bills can download your account activity. Within this list, you also find department store credit cards, discount membership warehouses, insurance companies, and even PayPal. Select a bank or credit card and you see your current account balance as well as a list of recent transactions.

Pageonce – Money & Bills also has access to a wide range of regional utility providers, as well cable and phone companies. For each account, you can see how much you owe and when your next payment is due. Depending on the vendor, more information may be available, such as in the figure on the right, where Pageonce – Money & Bills displays the usage statistics for my AT&T account (yes, I know, I've got *a lot* of roll-over minutes).

Two additional useful categories Pageonce – Money & Bills tracks are shopping and travel. Available companies under shopping include Amazon, eBay, and Wal-Mart. You can even access your Netflix account, but I'm not really sure why I need to see my Netflix Queue when I'm trying to manage my finances. Travel lets you track your rewards points and displays itineraries for upcoming trips. You can also add a number of social networking and e-mail accounts, but once again, I don't feel these really belong in this type of app. Despite the overkill, I suppose it's better to have access to too much information than not enough.

You can access all this information from a Web browser, by logging in at www.pageonce.com. In fact, while you can enter your account information in Pageonce – Money & Bills, I highly recommend instead first setting up access to each of your accounts using a browser on a computer. Doing the initial setup for your accounts this way is much easier and quicker. After you enter your accounts, they automatically show up the next time you launch the Pageonce – Money & Bills app.

Best features

Pageonce – Money & Bills puts automatic alerts in your device's status bar. These alerts inform you of things such as recent transactions and bills that are due soon.

Worst features

I find the ads at the bottom of the screen distracting, but I have a hard time justifying paying $7.00 for the paid version, Pageonce Pro – Money & Bills, just to get rid of the ads.

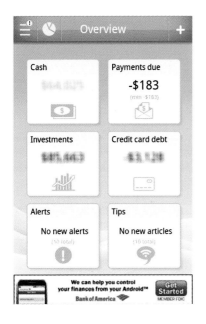

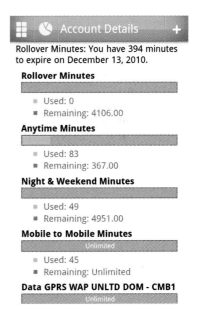

Checkbook
$1.99 US

Checkbook is a simple checkbook register app for managing your bank accounts and credit cards balances. To create an account, all you enter is the account's name and the starting balance. There's not much to entering transactions either: You input the amount of the transaction, designate whether it's a withdrawal or deposit, add an optional description (such as "check #124 to Mr. Roper for rent"), supply the date, and select whether you want it to appear as cleared or not in the register.

Checkbook includes one useful feature that I found lacking in most other free or similarly low-priced checkbook apps, and that is the capability to assign categories to each transaction (such as Cable Bill or Food) — you can even add you own custom categories. The one thing I wish Checkbook also would do, but does not, is to memorize repeat transactions. If that is important to you, then check out the $1.99 Ledgerist app.

Exchange Rates
Free

Exchange Rates is a very easy-to-use app that purports to provide up-to-the-minute exchange rates for "every world currency." As far as I could tell, this claim is true. Pick from an extensive list of currencies that you want to appear on the main screen. Each listed currency includes an image of the respective country's flag, the name of the country, and the currency's official three-letter code (such as ISK for the Icelandic Króna).

On the app's main screen, choose which of the listed currencies you want to use as the base currency. This is the currency that all the other currencies base their displayed exchange rates against. Long-tap any currency on the main screen to see a pop-up window with options such as viewing a currency chart or linking out to that currency's Wikipedia page.

Karl's Mortgage Calculator
Free (ad supported)

If you're shopping around for a mortgage, Karl's Mortgage Calculator is an invaluable tool for doing quick number crunching to see how much those mortgages are really going to cost you. Simply enter the principal, fixed or variable interest rate, and term, and the app shows you what your payments will be. You also can factor in your annual insurance and tax payments, and even add prepayments and extra payments to the mix. After you enter all the numbers, you can view a variety of tables and graphs that show the interest, principal, and balance due over time.

PayPal
Free

PayPal is the go-to means for paying for items and services online for many folks. The PayPal app makes it easy to manage your PayPal account from your Android device, allowing you to do things like add funds, withdraw money, and add credit cards to your account. You can also use the app to send money from your PayPal account or request payment from other people. Perhaps the coolest feature of the app, however, is that using PayPal's "Bump" technology, you can physically place your device next to someone else's device to transfer funds between your respective PayPal accounts. (This is much more secure than it sounds, as both devices have to be running the Bump module, and the connection must be manually approved by the users of both devices.) It's never been so easy to pay your friends for your share of the pizza without ever opening your wallet.

Yahoo! Finance
Free (ad supported)

I tend to think of Yahoo! Finance as "Bloomberg lite" (I also review the Bloomberg app in this chapter). Like Bloomberg, it dishes the top stories in the world of finance, displays the major stock indexes, tracks stocks, and enables you to look up information about companies. It doesn't have anywhere near the depth that Bloomberg does, but Yahoo! Finance's easy-on-the-eyes interface makes it a great choice when you want to take a quick peek at the world's financial affairs or see how your favorite stocks are doing. Yahoo! Finance also includes the latest videos from Yahoo!'s Tech Ticker Web site, which is dedicated to covering technology stocks and businesses in Silicon Valley.

7 Games

 ## Air Control
£1.99

Air Control is one of my favorite games, and to say it can be addictive is an understatement. The object of the games is to act as an air traffic controller, landing an increasing number of airplanes and helicopters, without causing any midair collisions. Trust me when I say it isn't as easy as it looks.

Choose from four different airport maps. Two of them (Green Fields and Desert River) each have two runways and one helipad. The Wings of History map has two runways and a Zeppelin landing pad (yes, I said Zeppelin). The Blue Ocean map is an aircraft carrier that has only one runway and two helipads — by far, this is the most difficult map. (The free version, Air Control Lite, doesn't let you play the Wings of History or the Blue Ocean maps, and it also has ads.)

Aircraft first show up on the edge of the screen as red warning marks and with audible alarms (except for Zeppelins, which appear as larger green warning marks). Within seconds, the actual aircraft appear flying in a random direction. Tap the aircraft and trace a route from the aircraft to the runway. Red planes can land only on the runway designated for red planes, and blue planes can land only on the runway reserved for blue planes. Helicopters land on helipads.

When you trace a flight plan, the aircraft's color fades, a faint line traces its intended route, and a clicking sound momentarily plays to confirm that it's headed for the correct runway. This helps you tell the difference between aircraft that are set to land and those that haven't been assigned a flight plan yet. At any time, you can select an aircraft and alter its flight plan.

 TIP

If you are the type to stack up planes, forever circling the airport, be forewarned that there is a limit to the length of the flight plan you can trace. Aircraft that aren't assigned flight plans or exceed the maximum distance of their traced routes will fly in a straight line until they hit the edge of the screen and then bounce back in a new direction.

Further complicating things is that different types of aircraft fly at different speeds; helicopters are excruciatingly slow. If aircraft get too close to each other, a midair collision alert sounds and the aircraft in danger are highlighted with red circles. Midair collision alerts appear only when aircraft are already close to each other, so you have very little time to react and remedy the situation. When aircraft collide, the sounds of crashing and breaking glass play, and the game is over.

The more aircraft that you land in a session, the faster new aircraft appear on the screen. What starts out as a seemingly easy game quickly becomes a challenge: You must keep up with assigning flight plans while avoiding midair collisions in an increasingly crowded sky. If this still isn't tough enough for you, tap the Fast-Forward button on the lower-left corner of the screen to momentarily speed things up.

Best features

In addition to the normal airplane maps, there are also two "Cargo" maps, where you can land a plane only if it matches the color or type of plane that just previously landed on that runway. Even with two runways, this gets difficult quickly as more airplanes with additional colors start showing up.

Worst features

I wish there were more airport maps.

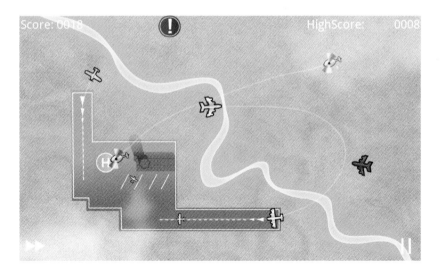

Angry Birds
Free (ad supported)

Angry Birds is an oddball take on the traditional cannonball game. Rather than lob cannonballs at your enemies, you hurl birds from a slingshot. And your enemies are green pigs. The pigs deserve these attacks because they stole the birds' eggs, which makes the birds very angry. So it's no wonder that the pigs seek shelter from the birds in jury-rigged fortresses made from glass, wood, and cinderblocks.

Each level begins with a peek at the pigs' current fortress. The fortresses range from flimsy affairs to seemingly impenetrable lairs. The pigs hide inside the fortress, on top of it, and sometimes even outside of it — some of the pigs aren't too smart. Pigs come in two sizes: small and large. The small ones are easy to destroy, but the bigger ones need a bit more force to get rid of (you can tell a pig is hurt, but not down for the count, by its black eyes). Sometimes the larger pigs wear helmets, which make them even harder to obliterate — some of the pigs are smarter than they look. When you wipe out a pig, it disappears in a puff of smoke.

When a bird is slung at the pigs' fortress, it often smacks into the fortress, knocking some of the pieces loose, sending parts of the fortress crashing down onto the pigs' heads. If a pig is hit hard enough by falling debris, it will be destroyed. A pig can also get zapped if a bird smacks directly into it. Often the only way to destroy all the pigs in a given level is to demolish the fortress on top of them piecemeal with repeated bird barrages. (If you get stuck on a particular level, you can find a number of "walkthroughs" online that show you how to obliterate all the pigs — sometimes with just one well-aimed bird.)

With each level you get a different number of birds, as well as different types of birds, to wield your destruction. If you run out of birds and pigs are still standing, you have to try the level over again in order to get a score. (Actually, the pigs don't appear to have legs, so they're doing whatever the equivalent of standing is for legless pigs.) When you launch a bird, you pull back on the slingshot and set the trajectory the bird should take. You can see the path the bird took, so you can adjust accordingly for the next salvo.

You get points for annihilating the pigs and for doing damage to their fortress. You get bonus points for any unused birds left over at the end of the level. The goal for many players is to get a score high enough on a level to earn three stars. Keep on racking up three-star scores and bonus levels become available.

Best features

By far the most fun aspect of Angry Birds has to be the different types of birds, each with special capabilities. The first bird you encounter is the Red Bird, who acts as a normal projectile. But soon you get to use the Blue Bird, who breaks up into three birds when you tap the screen. Yellow Birds speed up with a sudden jolt of acceleration when you tap the screen. Black Birds blow up, White Birds drop egg bombs, and Green Birds become boomerangs — all by tapping the screen at the right moment. Unfortunately, you can't just pick which bird to use. Each level assigns particular birds that you have to use in a specific order.

Worst features

There's very little to dislike about Angry Birds. Perhaps my only criticism is that some levels are excruciatingly difficult to get through.

 **Labyrinth**
£2.99

I have fond childhood memories of playing with my uncle's wooden labyrinth puzzle. The small box had two knobs on it that adjusted the tilt of the playing board on two axes. I tilted the board ever so slightly, this way and that, to guide a metal marble through a maze of walls, avoiding a minefield of holes, to the end of the maze. As satisfactory as it was to successfully navigate the maze, the puzzle got boring fairly quickly — it was always the same maze over and over again.

The Labyrinth Android app gives you access to an endless variety of mazes — from the super-easy to the absurdly difficult. Lest you think my use of the word "endless" is merely hyperbole, Labyrinth comes with more than 1,000 user-created mazes and you can download even more mazes directly on your Android device from a growing library. You can even create you own multilevel mazes on your computer (at edit.ilabs.nu) and send them to your device.

If you're just getting started, you might want to stick with one of the 50 "official" mazes before you explore others' sometimes very wacky creations. Ten "Easy" mazes help you get your feet wet.

To guide the marble through a maze, tilt your device left and right and back and forth. Labyrinth uses your device's built-in accelerometer to sense the orientation of the device and move the marble accordingly. Some older Android devices and low-cost Android tablets don't have accelerometers, so these devices won't be able to play Labyrinth.

 Before you play even one maze, go into the game's settings to calibrate how Labyrinth registers your device's accelerometer. Place your device on a flat surface, such as a table, wait for the bubbles in the onscreen carpenter's level to be centered, and then tap the Calibrate button, as the example in the figure on the right shows.

If you think £2.99 is too steep a price to pay for this game, try the free version, Labyrinth Lite, which comes with ten preset mazes and the capability to create up to ten mazes of your own. The Android Market has a handful of similar labyrinth puzzle games — some of which are cheaper or even free — but none of which, in my opinion, are as well polished as Labyrinth.

For a different take on a game that has you tilting your device to make marbles navigate a maze, check out the free (ad-supported) Graviturn Extended. This game introduces multiple, colored marbles — some of which you need to remove from the maze, while others must remain inside. Other features include black holes that capture marbles and maze walls that you can remove.

Best features

Labyrinth is a fun game to play and is also a great platform for showing off some of your Android device's advanced features. Go into the game's settings and turn on the Sound and Vibration settings. Now whenever the marble bounces off a wall, Labyrinth emits audio and vibrations that sound and feel like a real marble is hitting the actual wood wall of a maze. If you also turn on the 3D setting, the perspective of the maze's walls change, along with shadows, as you tilt your device. The level of realism you experience depends on the capabilities of your particular device.

Worst features

I wish there was a way to create new levels from within the Labyrinth app, instead of having to do so on my computer.

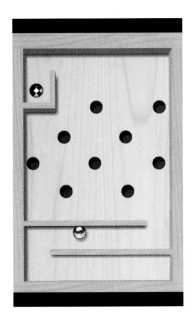
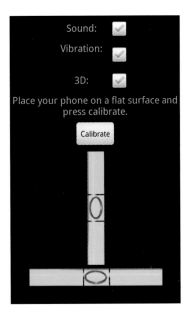

Real Blackjack
Free (ad supported)

You could dive right into Real Blackjack and start playing some virtual hands of twenty-one, but if you do, you'll miss a lot of what this robust card game offers. Real Blackjack is designed to help you hone your black-jack skills by mentoring you in a number of basic blackjack strategies.

The main screen looks like a real blackjack table, covered in green felt with the rules of the game written across the table. A dealer's shoe and a stack of chips sit at the top of the screen. When you start, you get $500 to use for betting. You can place bets anywhere between $1 and your entire virtual bankroll. If you want to add more money to your betting funds, tap the Menu button and then the Deposit button to add another $500 — tap the Deposit button repeatedly to add an additional $500 at a time. If only it was this easy to get money in the real world!

Tap the poker chips at the bottom of the screen to set your bet for the next deal. Then tap the Deal button to get your first two cards and to see the dealer's upcard. To draw another card, tap the Hit button or just tap your cards. If you don't want to draw another card, tap the Stand button or swipe your finger across your cards. Other available options are Surrender, Split Pairs, and Double Down. Once you stand, the dealer's hole card is turned over and more cards are dealt to the dealer, based on the "house" rules (the dealer draws on 16, but stands on 17 and higher).

Another useful option is the Advice button, which you can see in the figure on the left. Tap the Advice button, and it suggests what you should do based on the cards you've been dealt (such as Split Pairs, Stand, or Double Down). This advice comes from what Real Blackjack refers to as "Basic Strategy." If you want to see exactly what this strategy is, tap Menu and then tap the Basic Strategy button.

This opens up a detailed matrix, which you can see part of in the figure on the right. Based on what your hand's total is and what the dealer's upcard is, the table advises if you should hit (the green H in the figure), double down (the blue D), stand (the red S), or surrender (the brown R). Scroll down the table to see advice on what to do when one of your cards is an Ace (which is referred to as a "soft" hand, as the Ace can be counted as either a 1 or an 11), and whether to split when you are dealt a pair of cards that have the same value.

If you find any of this confusing, then you should probably check out the detailed Help screen, which is also available from the Menu button. The Help screen explains blackjack's basic rules, the card values, what your different options are when dealt a hand, and what the different card combinations mean, such as the difference between a soft hand and a hard hand.

Best features

Casinos don't all share the same rules, so Real Blackjack lets you adjust some of the rules. For instance, you can set the number of decks used in the dealer's shoe from one up to eight decks. Some other available settings are whether the dealer stands or hits on a soft 17, under what circumstances you can double down, and if surrendering your hand is an option.

Worst features

Maybe I'm just a sore loser, but it feels to me that the dealer wins too many games. The hands dealt are supposed to be random, but the sheer number of times that the dealer gets 20 or even blackjack is rather suspicious. I might not win many hands, but thanks to the plethora of Real Blackjack's information, at least I'm getting better at knowing why I'm losing.

Real BlackJack

4 - 8 DECKS in Shoe
Dealer stays on S17, Double Any 2 Cards, Double After Split, Surrender, US-Style (Dealer Peeks)

Estimated dealer edge for these rules: 0.36

Your hand	Dealer Upcard									
	2	3	4	5	6	7	8	9	10	A
Hard sums										
5	H	H	H	H	H	H	H	H	H	H
6	H	H	H	H	H	H	H	H	H	H
7	H	H	H	H	H	H	H	H	H	H
8	H	H	H	H	H	H	H	H	H	H
9	H	D	D	D	D	H	H	H	H	H
10	D	D	D	D	D	D	D	D	H	H
11	D	D	D	D	D	D	D	D	D	H
12	H	H	S	S	S	H	H	H	H	H
13	S	S	S	S	S	H	H	H	H	H
14	S	S	S	S	S	H	H	H	H	H
15	S	S	S	S	S	H	H	H	R	H
16	S	S	S	S	S	H	H	R	RS	R

Word Drop Pro
£0.69

I like games that make me think, and nothing seems to get the gears turning more than a good word game. Add a little strategy to the mix, and you get a game that keeps me entertained for hours.

Word Drop Pro fits that bill perfectly. Like many word games, Word Drop Pro lets you create words out of a random group of letters. Letters are assigned point values. Common letters like E are worth only one point, and less frequently used letters worth more points — up to ten points for letters like Q and Z. Each letter's value appears on the lower-right corner of the letter tile.

The goal is to accrue as many points as possible before the timer runs out. Words that are only two or three letters long are worth the total value of all of their letters' points added up. Longer words, however, are worth more. Four-letter words are given one and a half times their total points, and five-letter words get twice their face value. If you are brilliant and lucky enough to find an eight-letter word, it is worth ten times the sum of the points of its letters. Longer words also tack some extra time back onto the game clock.

Letters are laid out in a grid of tiles on the game board. (You can set the board as a 4x4, 5x5, or 6x6 grid of tiles.) Words can be formed from adjoining tiles, including tiles that are diagonally connected. In the figure on the left, you can see how I formed the word "WHAT." Select tiles by swiping a path through the letters, or by selecting them one at a time and then tapping the Submit Word button. Once your word is submitted, the tiles from that word disappear, the tiles that were sitting above slip down to take their place, and new tiles drop in from above.

 Strategy comes into play after you create a four-letter or longer word. At this point, a "combo multiplier" bonus appears on a random tile. If you manage to include that letter in your next word, your point total for that word doubles. A new combo multiplier then randomly shows up on a different tile, and if you use it, it boosts the word's score by three times. This keeps happening, with combo multipliers up to a five-times value. If you make a word that doesn't use a combo multiplier, the combo multiplier disappears and won't show up again until you create another word with at least four letters. The W in the word "WHAT" in the figure on the left has a four-times combo multiplier (the roman numeral, IV, in the upper-left corner).

If you struggle to make words from the jumble of letters, tap the Shuffle button, which yanks a random tile from each column and plunks it back at the top of the column it came from. If you still have trouble, tap the Discard button and a whole new set of tiles appears. (If you discard your tiles, any combo multipliers on the board go away too.)

Word Drop Pro's library of words is based on a Scrabble dictionary and Webster's New International Dictionary. Combined, Word Pro recognizes 153,136 words.

You can play Word Drop Pro in six different game modes, each with varying levels of difficulty. For a leisurely, no-pressure game session, play the Untimed mode.

Best features

You don't have to pay $0.69 to play this game. If you don't mind an ad banner running across the top of the screen, install the free Word Drop app from the Android Market.

Worst features

Words and strategy ... what's not to love?

Abduction! World Attack
£1.35

In Abduction! World Attack, you're a cow (nothing personal) and it's up to you save the rest of your herd, which has been abducted by aliens. In this vertical-scrolling game, you guide your cow up a series of platforms by tilting your Android device left and right. Along the way, you have the chance to earn points by catching members of your herd who are parachuting from the UFO — but avoid the parachuting bombs! You also encounter bonus opportunities on the way up — some will help you and some will hinder you — but you don't know what each bonus does until your cow touches it. If you miss a platform and fall to the bottom of the screen, it's game over for Bessie.

Abduction! World Attack features 22 levels and 54 timed challenges. Additional game modes become available after you complete all of the adventures and challenges. You can also fire up the Quick Game mode for an impromptu round that offers a variety of difficulty settings. Set to Kids, your cow merely bounces if she hits the bottom of the screen. Set to Medium or Hard, some of the platforms move. If you have lots of time on your hands, you can play the Infinite or Evil Infinite levels until the cows come home.

 # Bonsai Blast!
$1.99 US

Bonsai Blast is a shooter game, but what you're shooting are marbles. Perhaps it is this nonviolent approach that sets the game in a series of Zen-like gardens with serene music playing in the background. Stationed on a stone platform, you shoot marbles at a chain of colored marbles that slowly snakes its way down a path toward a Taijitu symbol (better known as a yin-yang symbol). You must eliminate all of the marbles in the chain before it reaches the end of the path. You do this by shooting a green marble at the green marbles in the chain, blue marbles at the blue marbles in the chain, and so on. When you shoot a marble at the chain, the marble is added to the chain. As soon as three or more marbles of the same color are next to each other, they disappear.

Bonsai Blast has more than 90 levels, which add increasingly difficult elements, such as shooting marbles through chutes and ricocheting marbles off walls. There is also a free version of Bonsai Blast, which includes ads. This might be the first game you ever played where you actually want to lose all of your marbles.

Jewellust
$2.95 US

Jewellust is similar to other jewel games: You swap the position of two adjacent jewels to create a string of three or more of the same color jewel. The longer the string, the more points you get. The string vanishes, and more jewels scroll down to fill the now vacant spaces. But the goal here is more than just to score as many points as possible before the clock runs out. Mixed in with the jewels are the fragments to a mosaic. You must manipulate the mosaic tiles to the bottom of the screen before time runs out, in order to make it to the next level in Campaign mode. Along the way, you earn bonuses that let you do things like zap an entire row of jewels or turn jewels from one color into another.

Mahjong 3D
Free (ad supported)

Mahjong 3D is a Mahjong solitaire game in which you have to find matching tiles and try to clear the board. In addition to having a snazzy-looking 3D interface that changes perspective as you alter your view of the board, you can also change the background color and choose from three different tile sets. My favorite feature of Mahjong 3D would have to be the 70 different possible tile formations from which to choose.

Shoot U!
$1.99 US

The point of Shoot U! is to shoot a rag doll out of a cannon and have it hit a red ball with a star on it. You can adjust the angle of the cannon as well as how much force it shoots with. Each level adds increasingly difficult challenges in the form of immovable obstacles like walls, and moveable objects, such as block, balls, and levers. Sometimes it takes several shots to move objects into the right spot or position multiple rag dolls in the playing field in order to hit the red ball. Part of what makes this game so appealing is that you have to abide by the laws of physics in order to reach your objectives. Also what makes Shoot U! fun is its simple-looking graphics, meant to look like a kid's line drawings. You can even customize the rag dolls by pasting photos of people's faces on them.

8 Health, Food, and Fitness

 AllSport GPS
$9.99 US

Many Android apps use GPS to track your outdoor workouts. Several of these apps are even free, such as CardioTrainer, which I discuss in this chapter. So why would you pay almost ten bucks for AllSport GPS? Because it does some things other apps simply can't do.

Like other outdoor fitness apps, AllSport GPS is meant to be used for activities such as running, cycling, and skiing. Its Stats page tracks things like your distance, average speed, and calories burned, and it enables you to customize which of these items appear on the page. The stats update in real-time during your workout.

The Map page shows your current location and a trail of where you've just been. The Charts page displays your elevation or speed, measured in distance or time.

One cool feature of AllSport GPS is the five different map views you can choose from, including street, aerial, topographical, hybrid (which combines map and street views), and terrain.

A unique aspect of AllSport GPS is how well it integrates with the Trimble Outdoors Web site (www.trimbleoutdoors.com). Your workouts are automatically uploaded to your Trimble Outdoors account, where you can edit your "trips" (that's what the site calls your workouts), analyze your stats, and even share your trips with the Trimble Outdoors community (which includes www.bicycling.com and www.backpacker.com). From these sites, you can view the trips that others have uploaded and made public. If you see a trip that you'd like to try, you can even add it to your account.

You can access the trips in your account from AllSport GPS, and download them to your Android device — this includes trips you add from other users, as well as trips you create using the tools on the Trimble Outdoors Web site. Downloaded maps display the complete route from the existing trip. You can use AllSport GPS's Follow Route or Race Against feature to follow this route or try to beat the time, respectively. AllSport GPS doesn't provide turn-by-turn directions, but you can visually follow the route on the map. This combined with the topographical map view is especially useful for hikers (see the example in the figure on the right).

In addition to sharing your trips with other users, AllSport GPS can post your trip to Facebook and Twitter. When you finish a workout, you are prompted to choose which (if any) of the three sites to upload the data.

Best features

With access to a treasure-trove of other users' trailblazing efforts, you have a seemingly endless source of downloadable trips to try out for your next workout.

Worst features

It would be awesome if the downloaded trips included turn-by-turn directions.

 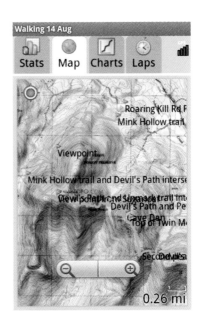

BigOven
Free (ad supported)

I am not a foodie. Until recently, most of what I ate came out of freezer bags, cans, and the occasional takeout container. But I found the more time I spent on BigOven, the social-networking recipe Web site (`www.bigoven.com`), the more inspired I became to change my ways. I started eating healthier, ate fewer processed foods, and spent more time in the kitchen, cooking (which, unfortunately, also meant more time in the kitchen cleaning). My wife still raves about a Bolognese sauce I made. So I was very excited when I discovered that there was a BigOven Android app and quickly installed it.

When I first launched BigOven, I was surprised to see a simple-looking design with a confusing user interface (UI). It definitely lacked the elegance of other more polished Android apps. You might momentarily be taken aback as well by its stark appearance, but don't let that deter you — there are over 170,000 user-submitted recipes here just waiting to be discovered, as well as a handful of useful features.

Every time you go to the BigOven home page, a large thumbnail image for a random recipe appears front and center — just like what's in the figure on the left. Tap the image and the full recipe opens in the window.

At the top of each recipe page are the overall user ratings and a description of the recipe, such as the figure on the right. Below that are tags that have been assigned to the recipe, such as "Bake" and "honey" in the recipe in the image for Polish Honey Cake. Next comes the actual recipe, broken out by ingredients and preparation.

BigOven works best when you have a free `BigOven.com` account. Assuming you do, you can take advantage of several options on every recipe page: Add to Favorites, Add to Try Soon, and I'm Making this Tonight! buttons. Tap these buttons to instantly add the recipe to your BigOven Favorites, Try Soon, and Recipes I've Made, lists, respectively. You can also e-mail the recipe to multiple recipients and save the ingredients to a grocery list. (As of December 2010, BigOven's grocery list feature became part of the BigOver Pro membership features, which costs $15.95 per year.) Each recipe includes ratings and comments by other BigOven users, and you can also rate and review the recipes.

If a recipe catches your eye, read the user comments. Many users provide valuable feedback on modifications they've made to improve the recipe or alter the ingredients' measurements in order to adjust serving size.

BigOven also includes a glossary for looking up food and cooking terms, and a What's for Dinner screen that displays a live feed of what BigOven users declare they're making for dinner tonight.

Quite a few other recipe apps are available for Android, but few have such a rich collection of recipes to choose from. Epicurious Recipe App (available in the Android market) was once one of the better ones, but at the time I wrote this, Epicurious Recipe was very buggy (electronically speaking) and kept crashing on many users (self included). Hopefully by the time you read this, the app's developers will have fixed the problems, and it will once again become as useful as BigOven.

Best features

I love BigOven's Leftover Wizard. Type in three ingredients, and BigOven returns with a list of recipes that incorporate all three items.

Worst features

One thing you can't do in the BigOven app that you can do on the BigOven.com Web site is upload a recipe.

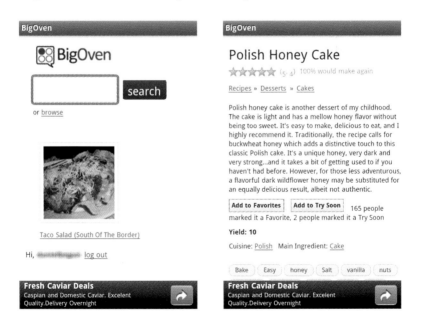

Calorie Counter by FatSecret
Free (ad supported)

The best way to lose weight is a healthy combination of exercise and eating right. At least that's what my mother always told me, and I'm going to give her the benefit of the doubt on this one. My biggest problem is portion control. Without even realizing it, I often consume far more calories than I need. But my scale has nothing to fear, for Calorie Counter by FatSecret is here!

Calorie Counter helps me figure out just how many calories are in that peanut butter and jelly sandwich I'm about to eat (450, as it turns out—see the figure on the left). Type in just about any type of food and Calorie Counter reports a wealth of nutritional information, such as total fat, protein, and percentage of Recommended Daily Intake (RDI). Calorie Counter even offers quick search lists based on food categories, restaurants and food chains, popular brands, and even supermarket brands (see the figure on the right). And if something isn't in Calorie Counter's database, you can add it.

But what good is all this information if you don't put it to use? You can keep a food diary within Calorie Counter, tracking every single morsel that goes down your gullet. Enter what you had for breakfast, lunch, dinner, and snacks, and Calorie Counter shows your daily nutritional intake.

You also can input your calorie-burning activities on an exercise diary. The time you invest in activities has to add up to 24 hours, so whatever time isn't spent sweating it off, is accounted for by resting and sleeping. The exercise diary subtracts any exercise time you add from one of those two activities.

Choose from plenty of pre-set activities, but you might not always agree with Calorie Counter's calorie-burning estimates. In those cases, add the activity as "Other" and supply your own description and estimate of calories you burned.

Once you start tracking your food intake and exercise, use Calorie Counter's Diet Calendar to track your progress. For each day you make entries, the Diet Calendar shows you a summary of how many calories you consumed, how many you exercised off, and what the net difference is. Did you burn off more than you ate? The bottom of the screen also shows your daily average and monthly total. If you want, you can also do a daily weigh-in; Calorie Counter displays a graph of your weight over time.

Create a free account on the FatSecret Web site (www.fatsecret.com), and then you can synchronize all your data between Calorie Counter and the site. The Web site offers more food, diet, and exercise options, and it lets you do even more things with your information.

Best features

By far, Calorie Counter's best feature is its built-in barcode scanner. Just point your device's camera at the barcode on practically any packaged food item, and it instantly pulls up all its nutritional information. If you eat packaged food, this makes entering meals into Calorie Counter ridiculously easy.

Worst features

Not all the nutritional information is accurate, so be sure to take it with a grain of salt.

CardioTrainer
Free

Whether you consider yourself a hardcore athlete or a recovering couch potato, CardioTrainer can track your workouts, help you schedule your workout routine, and even share your calorie-burning efforts with your friends.

Recording a workout is as simple as tapping the big green Start Workout button, which you see in the figure on the left. As soon as you do this, the screen changes to the workout screen, which shows a map of your current location and displays a few constantly updating stats, such as distance, speed, and how many calories you burn.

CardioTrainer knows these details because it uses your Android device's GPS to track your location. Obviously, CardioTrainer is best suited for outdoor exercises, such as walking, running, or cycling. You can use it to track your indoor workouts as well, but you won't have as much data to peruse afterwards. You can even manually add the details of any workouts that you didn't record on CardioTrainer while you were in the throes of all that activity.

If you like listening to tunes during your workout, CardioTrainer gives you two options. You can play your music using any app that supports multitasking, while CardioTrainer is running. Alternatively, you can enable CardioTrainer's Music Integration feature, which plays playlists created in Android's default Music app.

If you start hearing voices when using CardioTrainer, it probably isn't from dehydration. CardioTrainer includes spoken prompts that you can set to announce when you reach specific time or distance intervals. When the voice notification chimes in, it speaks over any music that is playing.

CardioTrainer automatically saves all your workouts, which you access from the History tab. Your workouts appear in a scrolling list, showing how long they lasted, how far you went, your average speed, and total calories burned (CardioTrainer estimates the last stat based on your body weight, which you plug into the app's settings).

 You also can set CardioTrainer to automatically send your workouts to the CardioTrainer Web site, where you can view them from a computer's Web browser using a special access code you find on the app's Settings page. You can also set CardioTrainer to post your workout results on your Facebook page.

A couple of premium add-ons are available for CardioTrainer to help you set weight-loss goals or race against your own previous workouts. The add-ons cost $2.99 each, but CardioTrainer includes 7-day trials for both add-ons if you want to take them for a spin before buying them. There's also a Pro version of CardioTrainer that adds six programs and 20 difficulty levels of interval training. You'll have to fork over $9.99 to try CardioTrainer Pro, but it comes with a 30-day money-back guarantee.

Best features

CardioTrainer can help you put together a weekly workout regimen. You can set CardioTrainer to display reminder notifications, and it even tracks whether you completed your planned workout (if you miss a scheduled workout, CardioTrainer doesn't have the option to accept lame excuses).

Worst features

Any complaint that I have about CardioTrainer would just be nit-picking. That said, here's my biggest nit-picking: It would be great if CardioTrainer could integrate a heart rate monitor. That would make my workout data complete.

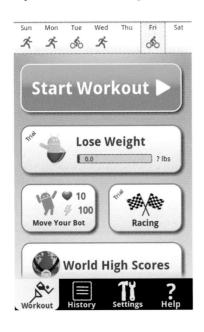

iTriage Mobile Health
Free

I'm not a doctor and have never played one on TV, so you probably don't want to take medical advice from me. But the two guys who first thought up iTriage Mobile Health are both ER physicians, so the wealth of health information in iTriage Mobile Health actually comes from the minds of true, trained medical professionals.

 Before I go any further, I have to state the obvious . . . Although you find plenty of useful medical information in iTriage Mobile Health, do not use it in place of advice from your own actual medical professional — especially during an emergency.

That said, iTriage Mobile Health can still be valuable during an emergency. Not to diagnose a life-threatening illness or learn how to deliver a baby (is there a *For Dummies* book for that?), but to help get you to the nearest medical facility. Tap the Find Medical Treatment button on iTriage Mobile Health's home page, and you can search for nearby medical facilities. You can choose from locations, such as emergency departments, urgent-care facilities, and pharmacies. If you select a facility and tap its address, Google Maps opens and displays the location. Use Google Maps to give you turn-by-turn directions. Also use iTriage Mobile Health to search for doctors based on their specialties.

But remember, in a true emergency, your safest bet is to call 911. And as it turns out, you can do that in iTriage Mobile Health as well, by tapping the Emergency button in the lower-right corner of the home page (see the figure on the left).

When you look at the record for a medical facility or health-care provider, some entries include links to where you can read detailed profiles and reviews of the facility or provider. In some cases, you can even submit your own review.

I mostly use iTriage Mobile Health to look up symptoms. Select one of the 300 or so symptoms in the database, such as *ankle pain,* and you see a list of potential causes. Tap one of the possible causes, and you next see a screen that looks like one in the figure on the right, which provides a bunch of resources to get more information or seek treatment.

If you want to learn more about a particular disease, iTriage Mobile Health has information on 1,000 of them. I didn't even know there were that many diseases. If you are a hypochondriac, this is probably not the section you want to read (or is it?).

Lastly, you can also use iTriage Mobile Health to learn about medical procedures. In addition to a short description of the procedure, you can learn about possible complications and find a specialist who can treat you.

iTriage Mobile Health is a rather unique application. No other Android apps out there come close to the breadth of medical information that iTriage Mobile Health provides. On the Internet, WebMD (`www.webmd.com`) is a similarly excellent source of medical information, but as of when I wrote this, WebMD hadn't released an official Android app.

Best features

Instead of tapping all those buttons and typing in all that text, just touch the Voice Search button and speak what you are searching for.

Worst features

The one critical topic that iTriage Mobile Health is missing is medications. It contains information related to medication abuse, overdoses, and poisoning, but it lacks detailed information, such as warnings, side effects, and interactions. For that level of information, check out Epocrates, on the next page.

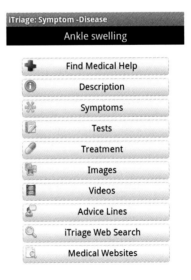

Epocrates
Free

Geared toward people working in the medical profession, Epocrates provides detailed information about more than 3,500 brand-name and generic medications. But this free app can also be a valuable tool for informed consumers. For all medications, Epocrates lists adult and pediatric doses, black box warnings, contraindications, adverse reactions, drug interactions, pricing, and much more. Epocrates has a wizard that checks for interactions with up to 30 different medications at a time. Another wizard helps you identify pills by their physical characteristics, such as shape, color, and imprint (the writing on the pill).

Medical students should find the built-in reference tables and medical calculators especially useful.

First Aid
Free (ad supported)

This is one app that you probably hope you'll never have to use. The aptly named First Aid offers detailed tips about what to do in a variety of traumatic and emergency medical situations. First Aid explains the possible signs for a particular ailment, such as head injuries or poisoning, and explains how to treat it. Many of the listed treatments even include links to informative YouTube videos. First Aid also tries to set the record straight on a number of common treatment myths, such as putting butter on a burn ("useless") or placing a bleeding wound under running water (it washes away clotting agents, allowing the wound to keep bleeding). First Aid also includes a list of items that you should include in your own first-aid kit. Lastly, a Test section quizzes you on how to deal with a variety of emergency situations.

Gentle Alarm
€1.99

For me, sleeping is easy. Waking up is the hard part. But Gentle Alarm has made that experience a little less tedious, by gently easing me awake in the mornings. Gentle Alarm recognizes that the sleep cycle alternates between light and heavy sleep. You can set a pre-alarm to lightly sound half an hour before the main alarm. If you are in a light sleep, the alarm will awaken you and you should arise feeling refreshed.

If you are in a deep sleep, you may sleep through the alarm; then 30 minutes later, when you're probably in a light sleep, the main alarm sounds. The alarm first plays at a soft level, and then slowly fades up to full volume. You can use your MP3 files, playlists, and ringtones as your alarm sounds. A free trial version with full functionality is available, but it doesn't play on Wednesdays. I never liked Wednesdays anyway.

 ## Jefit
Free

You don't have to be a muscle-bound weight lifter to get a lot of benefit from Jefit. The app comes preloaded with set workout routines that work different muscle groups on different days. You can add, delete, and edit the routines, as well as change the days of your workouts. Choose from plenty of exercises, which include simple animations (downloadable as a free plug-in) that show the beginning and end points of every exercise. You can even add your own exercises. During your workout, specify the weight and number of reps for each exercise you complete, and then Jefit automatically moves on to the next set or exercise. Later, check the log to see your past workout sessions.

 You can sync your workout data between the Jefit app and the Jefit Web site (www.jefit.com) for access to manage your workout routines online.

 ## White Noise
$1.99 US

With a catalog of 40 ambient sounds to choose from, White Noise can instantly transform a chaotic environment into a calm oasis. Tune out the rest of the world and relax to sounds such as Amazon (the river, not the retailer), Light Rain, or Wind. If you want to drift off to sleep to the sound of Cat Purring cat, a Tibetan Bowl, or even an Air Conditioner, you can set a timer so that the audio will turn off after the specified interval. White Noise supports multitasking, so the audio keeps playing while you run other apps. A free version, White Noise Lite, is available, but it includes only ten sounds and it doesn't support multitasking.

9 Music

Top Ten Apps

- doubleTwist Player
- Ringdroid
- Slacker Radio
- SoundHound
- TuneWiki Social Media Player
- Amazon MP3
- BeyondPod Podcast Manager
- Ethereal Dialpad (synthesizer)
- Old Timer Radio Player
- Scanner Radio

 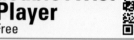

doubleTwist Player
Free

doubleTwist Player has all the features you expect from an audio player. View the audio files stored on your device by artist, album, song, or playlist. When you play a song, you can fast-forward, rewind, and skip to any spot in the track. You can shuffle your songs, repeat the track, or repeat your current playlist. With just a couple of taps, you can even turn the song you are listening to into a ringtone. You can even use doubleTwist to listen to podcasts and watch videos.

 Android devices with third-party user interfaces (UI) that sit on top of the Android OS — such as the HTC Sense UI found on virtually all HTC phones — can cause a little havoc with some media players, such as doubleTwist. These media players can "see" only the music files stored on an SD card, and not those in the device's internal storage. So if you wonder why your collection of Air Supply hits isn't appearing in doubleTwist Player, it isn't because your device is expressing its opinion of your musical tastes.

At this point, you're probably wondering, what's so "amazing" about doubleTwist? Plenty of media player apps do pretty much the same things. doubleTwist appears in this chapter, not so much for what the doubleTwist Android app can do, but because of the power of the Windows and Mac versions of the doubleTwist software. There's no easier way to sync audio files from your computer to your Android device — doubleTwist has often been called "iTunes for Android." Download doubleTwist for your computer from www.doubletwist.com.

Launch doubleTwist on your computer, plug in your Android device, and it appears in doubleTwist's Devices section. Once connected, you can transfer music, playlists, video, and pictures between your computer and your device. doubleTwist can also access the contents of your computer's iTunes music library and import your iTunes playlists. If you install the $4.99 doubleTwist AirSync plug-in on your device, you can instead transfer files between your device and computer over a Wi-Fi connection.

After you get doubleTwist set the way you like, you can set it to automatically sync your media files when you connect your device to your computer. The doubleTwist software also includes a podcast search tool and direct access to the Amazon MP3 store.

Both the Windows and Mac versions of doubleTwist have one more nifty feature: You can browse and search the Android Market for apps, directly from your computer. You can't install the apps to your device using doubleTwist, but you can use a barcode scanner app on your device to scan the onscreen QR Code. The QR Code is the square-looking blob, which acts as a link directly to an app's entry in the Android Market.

Best features

Super-easy way to automatically sync your music, playlists, and podcasts from your computer.

Worst features

Too often music makes it to the device without any album art. doubleTwist needs an album art importer, like TuneWiki (which I discuss later in this chapter).

Ringdroid
Free

Ringdroid is a free audio-editing app that lets you take audio files stored on your Android device's SD card, trim them down to shorter clips, and then save the resulting audio as ringtone, notification, or alarm audio files. You even have the option of saving edited audio files as music files. You can do this in as few as four taps on the screen.

If your device can play it, Ringdroid can edit it . . . *almost.* You can play 3GPP (AMR), AAC, MP3, MP4, WAV, and WMA audio files on Android devices, and Ringdroid can read and edit all of these audio files types except for WMA.

Here's how to make your custom ringtone in just four taps:

1. **Tap #1: Launch Ringdroid.**

2. **Tap #2: Tap the entry for the audio file you want to turn into a ringtone.**

   When Ringdroid launches, it displays a list of all the audio files stored on your device's SD card. Scroll down the list until you find the audio file you want. (I'm not counting this scrolling as a tap.)

   You can also search for an audio file instead of finding it in the list, but then that would require more than four taps, wouldn't it?

3. **Tap #3: Tap the Save button on the editing screen.**

   After you select an audio file, it opens in the editing screen, which you can see in the figure on the left. Ringdroid automatically edits the clip down to its first 15.05 seconds. Tapping the Save button at this point opens the Save As dialog box (which I'll touch upon in just a moment in Step 4).

   If you don't want the first 15 seconds of the audio file, however, you're going to have to do a bit more tapping. Adjust the sliders to where you want the clip to start and end. Zoom in for tighter control of the start and end points. Tap the Play button to hear what the clip will sound like. When you've got it the way you want it, go ahead and tap the Save button.

4. **Tap #4: Tap the Save button in the Save As dialog box.**

   By default, Ringdroid wants to save the clip as a new ringtone file. Tapping the Save button here saves the ringtone file to your device's SD Card.

   Voilà! You now have a new ringtone.

You also have the option of saving the edited audio file as a Music, Alarm, or Notification audio file. You can also edit the name of the file that Ringdroid will save, if you're not happy with the filename that Ringdroid automatically picked.

Another cool thing Ringdroid can do is record your voice or capture any audio from your device's microphone and turn that into a ringtone, alarm, notification, or music file. The Recorder screen shows in the figure on the right.

I'm no lawyer, but I must point out that you could be violating the copyright of any commercial recording that you turn into a ringtone. If the RIAA (Recording Industry Association of America) comes knocking on your door, don't blame me!

Best features

Many audio player apps let you turn songs into ringtones, but none of them let you do so with this much control of the exact portion of the song you want to use.

Worst features

After Ringdroid saves a recording, the app automatically quits. If you want make more ringtones, you have launch the app again.

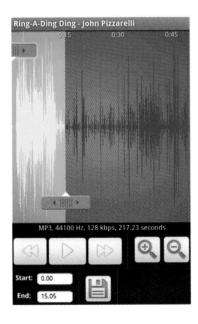

Slacker Radio
Free (ad supported)

Slacker Radio lets you listen to whatever music you want to hear, whenever you want to listen. Really. In the mood for hard rock? Slacker Radio's got it. Want to hear some smooth jazz? No problem. Craving holiday music in August? Whatever floats your boat!

Slacker is the sort of service commonly known as *streaming music* or *music discovery*. Similar services are Pandora Radio and Last.fm (both available as free apps in the Android Market). Here's how it works: You specify a music genre or artist, and Slacker Radio starts playing songs from that genre or artist. If you pick an artist, Slacker Radio mixes in songs from other similar artists. For instance, if you pick The Beatles, Slacker Radio might also play songs from The Kinks, The Doors, and other artists from that era. That's the "discovery" part — by listening to similar artists, you potentially learn about new artists and songs.

When you hear a song you like, select it as a favorite. If you don't like it, you can "ban" either the song or the artist. The more you do this, the more Slacker Radio picks songs that you likely want to hear. If you like what you hear, you can save it as a favorite station, so it's easy to play again whenever you want — it becomes your own personal radio station. If you're really excited about the station and want to share it, Slacker Radio lets you send out invitations to your friends to hear the station, via e-mail, text message, Facebook, or Twitter.

You can look at information about a song when it's playing. This includes an artist's biography, a review of the album (as the example in the figure on the right shows), and the first few lines of the song's lyrics. (Lyrics aren't available for all songs, but you'll be surprised just how many popular tracks include lyrics.)

If you don't like the song you're listening to, just tap the Skip Ahead button and Slacker Radio instantly moves on to the next song. You can skip ahead only six times per hour for any given station.

If you want to skip ahead as many times as you like, you must spring for a Slacker Radio Plus subscription, which costs $4.99 per month. A subscription gives you other benefits as well, such as no audio or banner ads, the complete lyrics for songs (when lyrics are available), and an ABC News feed.

Best features

A Slacker Radio Plus subscription gives you what I think is the cool-est feature of the app: You can "cache" your stations, so that you can listen to them offline. This means that your stations will be avail-able even when your device doesn't have an Internet connection. You're limited by the available memory on your SD card, but my HTC Incredible's 2GB SD card can hold up to 25 stations. Cached stations automatically refresh when your device is charging. You can also force a manual refresh at any time. One advantage of caching stations is that if you have spotty service, you don't have to worry about the audio momentarily stopping while the stream buffers. Also, playing audio from the SD card consumes less battery power than streaming it over a network connection.

Worst features

On the Slacker Web site (www.slacker.com), you can further cus-tomize a station by tweaking a number of Fine Tune options and edit a station by requesting specific songs and artists. Regretfully, you don't have this level of control with the Slacker Radio Android app.

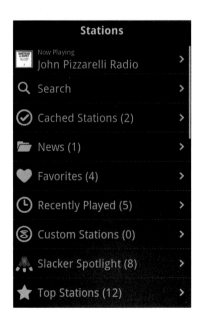

SoundHound
Free (ad supported)

I can't even count the number of times I've been somewhere when I hear a song playing and I feel the need to know who's singing. Well, I can name that tune in as little as four seconds . . . with a little help from SoundHound.

All I need to do is face my Android device's microphone toward the source of the music and tap SoundHound's big orange What's That Song? button (see the figure on the left). SoundHound immediately starts streaming the audio it hears from the microphone over the Internet to a server that analyzes the audio against a huge database of music, and then sends the results back to SoundHound within seconds.

You might be familiar with a similar Android app called Shazam, which is available in the Android Market. SoundHound and Shazam do the same thing, but SoundHound has far more useful features than Shazam offers.

I'm amazed at how quickly and accurately SoundHound identifies the songs it hears. The one song I've found that can stump SoundHound is one of my daughter's favorites, "Elmo's Song." But I don't really need SoundHound to tell me who sings that. I also find SoundHound does a better job at identifying music that has lyrics.

 You can use SoundHound even if your device doesn't have a signal. Your searches will be saved in the History section (SoundHound saves all of its searches). The next time your phone has a signal, tap SoundHound's History button, and then tap any entries that say Pending Search.

If you've got a song in your head that you can't quite place, just sing or hum it into SoundHound and it might actually figure out what the song is. Trying to use this feature just reinforced for me that I can't carry a tune to save my life, as SoundHound had little luck indentifying *any* of the songs that I sang or hummed. But I've seen plenty of other folks with better sounding voices than mine have much better luck with this feature.

You can also search for song titles or artists by tapping the Title or Artist box and saying what you are looking for. If you don't feel like talking to your device, you can also just type in your search. When I searched for "Elmo's Song" this way, SoundHound found it.

 In addition to song titles and artists, when you search by typing, the results include lyrics (if available) and albums.

Your search results may produce no matches, a list of possible matches, or an exact match. When you get a match, the results screen shows you the song title, who sang it, which album it's on, and the album cover art. You can save the results as a bookmark, share them with your friends, or buy the track from the Amazon MP3 store.

You can also look up the song's lyrics, find out if there are any related YouTube videos, view a list of similar artists, and discover which other albums the song appeared on. For some songs, you can even hear a 30-second snippet of the track.

Best features

SoundHound is ridiculously easy to use, and it's great at instantly satisfying your impulsive need to know everything about a song that's playing at that very moment.

Worst features

The free version of SoundHound limits you to only five searches per month via the big orange button (there's no limit on the other types of searches). Even incorrect results count against your monthly quota — and there's no way to tell SoundHound when it's wrong. For $4.99, you can purchase SoundHound Infinity, which gives you unlimited searches from the big orange button and removes ads.

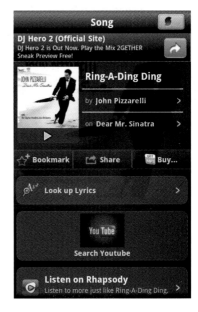

TuneWiki Social Media Player
Free (ad supported)

After looking at the title of this app, you might be asking, "What exactly is a 'social media player'?" How does it play social media?!? It doesn't. It's a media player that uses the power of social networking. To clear up any future confusion, I propose the app instead be called the "TuneWiki Media-Player with Social-Networking Goodness." Okay, maybe not — but you get my point.

For starters, TuneWiki has all the normal media player necessities for playing music and videos stored on your device's SD card. But as soon you start playing music, TuneWiki's unique capabilities begin making their appearance. As a song plays, its lyrics scroll up the screen in time with the audio. See an example of this in the figure on the left. You'll probably encounter lots of songs that don't have lyrics, but for those that do, it's your chance to sing along and finally get the words right.

Lyrics are available in more than 40 languages. The lyrics are submitted, translated, and edited by the TuneWiki community. If you want to contribute lyrics to a song, however, you have to do so on TuneWiki's Web site (www.tunewiki.com) — you can't do this from within the TuneWiki app.

While a song is playing, you can send out SMS, e-mail, Twitter, or Facebook messages (TuneWiki calls these "Blips"), announcing what you are listening to, as well as a link to the song's page on the TuneWiki Web site. You can also see if the song is included in any YouTube videos. If you're lucky, you might even find footage of the song being performed live. If the lyrics appeared during audio playback, you see them during video playback as well.

TuneWiki includes a few more built-in community features. You can search for user-submitted lyrics by artist, song title, or phrase. If you are searching for a popular song, you'll likely see a long list of user submissions. If you take a gander at a few of them, you'll probably see some minor variations between them — owing to a particular artist's version of a song or sometimes indicating that the lyrics aren't always 100 percent accurate. Then again, I get song lyrics wrong all the time, so maybe I'm not the best judge of accuracy here.

If you want to know what other TuneWiki users are listening to, you've got a few options. You can see maps of TuneWiki users all over the world. The figure on the right shows the TuneWiki listeners who were in my neck of the woods on a particular day. Zoom into any area and you can tap the icon for a user to see what she or he is listening to. Apparently, Lady Gaga and Britney Spears have fans in Beijing.

Another way to see what's popular is to look at the TuneWiki Charts. You can see who the top 50 artists are for the day, week, or month. Select an artist and a list of that performer's top 50 songs appears. Tap the song title and it launches a YouTube video.

You can also see the top 50 songs for all TuneWiki users worldwide, or just for specific countries. These lists break down by day, week, and month as well. It seems that Lady Gaga is also big in Japan.

TuneWiki includes two more ways you can discover new music: You can listen to tunes from both the Last.fm and SHOUTcast Radio audio streaming services. If you have a Last.fm account, you can even set TuneWiki to "scrobble" what you listen to (this means that Last.fm collects information about what you listen to in order to build a more accurate profile of your musical tastes).

Best features

Many users appreciate TuneWiki's scrolling lyrics and its social networking features. My favorite feature is the Album Art Manager, which helps fetch missing cover art for music files.

Worst features

You're likely to be disappointed by the YouTube videos. Many of them are just static images or have user-supplied content that just uses the audio track as their soundtracks.

Amazon MP3
Free

Amazon MP3 is quite possibly the easiest way to purchase music directly on your Android device. Search the store, browse by genre, and see the current bestselling albums and songs. If you're looking for deals, you'll find them right on Amazon MP3's home page as the Free Song of the Day and the Album Daily Deal (which is the day's deeply discounted album). Tap almost any song to hear a 30-second preview. Download songs or albums to your Android device's SD card. And since the MP3 files you download don't use copy protection, you can copy them off your device and play them on any other device or computer that plays MP3 files.

BeyondPod Podcast Manager
$6.99

To say that BeyondPod Podcast Manager is merely a podcast manager is like claiming that a Ferrari is just a car. In addition to managing audio podcasts subscriptions, the app also manages your RSS feeds and Video podcast subscriptions—and it seamlessly integrates with your Google Reader account (if you have one). Assign your feeds to categories, and then set specific update schedules for each category to automatically download the feeds to your device. Depending on the quality of your Internet connection, some podcasts can be streamed without first needing to be downloaded. You can also create playlists or let BeyondPod Podcast Manager's SmartPlay feature auto-generate a playlist for you, based on your preferences.

Ethereal Dialpad ### (synthesizer)
Free

Musicians and non-musicians alike can get a lot of enjoyment from the Ethereal Dialpad touch synthesizer. Just tap the display or drag your finger across the screen to generate some truly trippy-sounding music. You can alter the synthesizer's sound by playing with the Pitch quantizer, Octaves, and various other effects settings. I only wish the app would let me record my musical creations.

Make sure to also install the free Dialpad: NightSky plug-in, which lets you use two fingers on the screen simultaneously to create music.

Old Timer Radio Player
Free (ad supported)

I'm a huge fan of old-time radio (OTR) — also known as the Golden Age of Radio. These radio shows aired long before I was born, but I've had the privilege of hearing many of the original broadcasts that my parents listened to growing up — shows like *Fibber McGee and Molly,* *The Lone Ranger,* and *The Shadow.* If you haven't heard these old radio shows, you should really give them a listen — they'll truly transport you into the past. Finding these old shows is as simple as installing Old Timer Radio Player and selecting them from the listed genres (there is no search function). After you choose a show, it starts playing in just a few seconds; it also downloads to your device's SD card as an MP3 file, so you can listen to it later, or even copy it from your device to your computer. A lot of great content is available, but I wish there were even more shows to listen to!

Scanner Radio
Free (ad supported)

It used to be that the only people who listened to scanners were news hounds, career criminals, and scanner buffs. The scanners were so expensive that only those select groups could justify the expense. These days, many police, fire, and EMS radio frequencies stream live over the Internet, so anyone can eavesdrop on what his or her community's public safety workers are up to. Thanks to Scanner Radio, you can also listen in using your Android device. Scanner Radio includes audio from more than 2,300 feeds around the world, including air, marine, and rail radio communications. To find local communications, tap the Scanners Near Me button to see all the available nearby frequencies. If you want to get rid of the ads, you can buy Scanner Radio Pro for $2.99. One word of warning: If you find yourself humming the theme from the TV show *Cops* while monitoring scanner frequencies, you might be enjoying it a bit too much.

10 News and Weather

Engadget
Free

Engadget is one of the top Web destinations for the latest tech news and up-to-the-minute information about the hottest gadgets. If you're a frequent visitor to the Engadget Web site (www.engadget.com), you'll feel right at home with the Engadget Android app. And if you are just getting your geek feet wet, Engadget is a great place to get started.

When you first launch Engadget, you have the option of looking at content pulled from the Engadget site (for all things tech), the Engadget Mobile site (for mobile tech), the EngadgetHD site (for audio/visual tech), or the Engadget Alt site (for tech news that's on the quirky side of things). After you pick one, it becomes the default selection whenever you subsequently launch the app. Not to worry, though, as it's easy enough to change this in the settings.

Tabs on the bottom of the screen provide access to five different pages. The Latest tab displays a page with the most-recent headlines, which appear in a scrolling list; you can see an example in the figure on the left. If you reach the bottom of the page and want to see more stories, tap the Next button, and a new page loads. Each story in this list displays a headline, a small thumbnail image, and the time and date the story posted. Tap any item in the list to see the full story. If you are more interested in a specific subject, tap the Topics tab and pick from a list that includes topics like Cameras, Gaming, and Laptops.

The Videos page lists current and previous episodes from the monthly Engadget video show, which is popular among the geek set. The Engadget gang also does a weekly podcast, which you find on — you guessed it — the Podcasts page. Select any video or podcast, and in a few seconds your selection starts streaming to your device. What you won't see in the list of videos, however, are any of the numerous other videos from the Engadget Web site, such as unboxing of brand new products and video product reviews. If you want to see these other videos from your Android device, you have to track them down on YouTube.

Engadget's last page is Galleries, and it includes a plethora of photos of new tech products. In the example in the figure on the right, the displayed page is one of 434 pages — and each page has nine galleries, and each gallery contains multiple photos. That's a lot of images! If it's gadget and tech news you want, Engadget's got it.

Best features

I have yet to find another Android app that comes close to delivering the breadth of coverage and detail of gadget and tech goodness that Engadget does.

Worst features

Engadget doesn't support multitasking. When watching videos or listening to podcasts, don't exit the Engadget app to do anything else, like check e-mail, because playback will instantly cease. If you want to listen to Engadget podcasts while doing other tasks on your device, use a dedicated podcast app like BeyondPod Podcast Manager (which I discuss in the Music chapter).

 **NPR News**
Free

When it comes to getting in-depth, thought-provoking news, it's tough to beat National Public Radio (NPR). And with the NPR News app, NPR fans can listen to many of their favorite NPR shows while on the go. Even better, NPR News enables you to listen to live broadcast streams from many of NPR's local affiliate stations — perhaps even your local NPR radio station. For instance, five out of the six NPR stations in my area offer live streams.

To find an NPR station, tap the Stations selection on the NPR News home page (see the figure on the left). You'll be asked if you want to find a station based on your current location, by zip code, or by a station's call sign. All the stations that meet your search criteria are listed, and a small icon that looks like a red speaker appears next to the entry for every station that has audio you can listen to.

 Just because the audio icon appears next to a station does not necessarily mean that the station's live broadcast is available for streaming. In some cases, podcasts are the only available audio choices for a station.

Many stations offer both live streams and podcasts. The podcasts are typically from shows that the station produces itself — as opposed to the national or syndicated content the station also probably airs. The podcasts can be just a short clip, like a news segment, or a full-length show.

After you start listening to a podcast or live broadcast stream, it appears in an audio player that slides up from the bottom of the screen (see the figure on the right). You can add additional podcasts to the playlist so that as soon one finishes, the next one automatically starts playing. NPR News supports multitasking; when you leave the app to do something else on your device, the audio keeps playing.

If you want to listen to one of the national or syndicated NPR shows, you find them in the Programs section. Many of NPR's popular shows are available, such as *All Things Considered, Weekend Edition,* and my personal favorite, *Wait, Wait . . . Don't Tell Me!* Sadly, one of my other favorites, *Car Talk,* is not available.

When you select a Program to listen to, the entire broadcast does not appear as a single listing. Instead, each broadcast is broken down into multiple segments. So if you want to listen to an entire broadcast, you manually have to add each segment to the playlist.

In addition to audio, NPR News includes text-based news stories (with photos). These stories — which are often very detailed and lengthy — are in the Top Stories and Topics sections. These two sections include a mix of audio and text news stories. Also, if you are interested in a particular subject, you can use the Search feature to see if NPR has covered it.

Best features

NPR's broad range of in-depth, news programming — including expansive coverage of the arts, politics, science, and much more — offers something for everybody.

Worst features

When I first looked at the NPR News app, it was a little buggy. Subsequent versions behaved better, but plenty of users were still complaining about issues they were having with the app on their devices. So before you decide to rely on it as your sole news source, spend a little time with the NPR News app to see how it behaves on your device.

NubiNews Reader
Free

To get a truly balanced view of the world's happenings, you need to get your news from more than just a single source; but it can be troublesome and time-consuming to hunt down all the different news sources you might want to read. Wouldn't it be great if all those sources could come to you? Well, they can in the form of an RSS (Really Simple Syndication) reader app, like NubiNews Reader.

If you are not familiar with RSS, it is a means that many Web sites and blogs use to disseminate their content over the Internet as published "feeds." Users then subscribe to multiple feeds using RSS reader applications, of which there are many.

While NubiNews Reader is an RSS reader, where it really stands out is as a true news aggregator. NubiNews Reader comes with a long list of mainstream news sources already built in. These include well-respected news organizations such as the BBC, CNN, and *The New York Times.* You can see a small selection of some of the built-in news sources in the figure on the left. NubiNews Reader is optimized to display the feeds from these built-in sources, so that they load quickly and are easy to read on the screen. (RSS feeds can be notoriously slow to load and difficult to display correctly.) The developer of this app is not sitting idly by — regular updates continue to incorporate additional optimized news sources.

In addition to the built-in RSS feeds, you can add any other RSS feeds you want. The feeds you add, however, might not load as quickly or look as good as the built-in feeds. To add your own RSS feed, you need to know the RSS feed's Web address (URL). When you add an RSS feed, first tap the Select Feeds tab on the My RSS Feeds page to see if the feed is already listed in the developer's list of RSS feeds that have been tested (but not optimized) with NubiNews Reader.

NubiNews Reader can also access your Google Reader feeds. The experience isn't quite as seamless as it is with the NewsRob app (which I discuss in this chapter), or even when you access Google Reader directly from your Android device's Web browser (`google.com/reader/i`), but all your Google Reader content is accessible.

When you access your Google Reader feeds with NubiNews Reader, you first see a list of all your Google Reader sources, and then have to select a source to see the stories within that feed. When you access Google Reader in a Web browser, though, the default view displays the latest stories collected from all your various feeds — I prefer this approach much better. But NubiNews Reader's developer considers this a beta feature of the app, so I wouldn't be surprised to see this addressed in updates. The developer is highly receptive to suggestions from NubiNews Reader's users, so if you would like to see a feature added, ask for it.

One NubiNews Reader feature I really like is the capability to download feeds for offline reading. If I know my device is going to be without Internet access for a while — such as when I'm on the subway — I can save the feeds ahead of time that I know I'm going to want to read.

NubiNews Reader is a robust app with a lot of user-selectable options for how it operates — it is a great RSS reader option for power users. But even the less technically minded should find its straightforward interface easy to use. And even if you never add any feeds other than the ones that are already built in, NubiNews delivers a wealth of news from a wide variety of reliable sources.

Best features

The developer regularly updates NubiNews Reader — often incorporating features suggested by users. The app keeps getting better and better.

Worst features

It needs more robust Google Reader features.

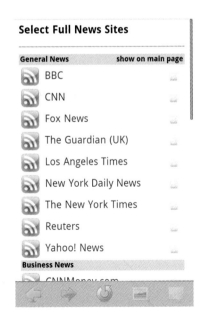

USA Today

Free (ad supported)

I'm a self-admitted news junkie. I'm constantly checking the latest headlines to see what's happening in the world — even when I'm on the go. Luckily, USA Today delivers all the news that's fit to read. Truthfully, there's no shortage of decent general-news apps available for Android devices; but USA Today manages to beat out the others with its elegant design and easy-to-navigate interface.

USA Today divvies up information into five separate tabs at the top of the screen: Headlines, Scores, Weather, Pictures, and Snapshots. Anything that's considered "news," you find under the Headlines tab, where the stories appear in a scrolling list. In addition to a headline, you see the first two lines of a story and a related photo. Tap an entry and the entire story opens, along with a photo. Tap a photo and it fills the screen.

The Headlines section breaks the day's news down into bite-size categories, such as Top News, News, Money, and Sports. The Top News category shows the latest breaking news stories. The News category is actually similar to Top News, and you even see some of the same stories in both sections; but the News section includes a nifty little Subsection button that lets you narrow down the stories based on subcategories, such as Nation, World, or Religion. In fact, all of the Headlines news categories (other than Top News) include a Subsection button. For example, the figure on the left shows the Subsection button for Sports news. Tap this button and you can look at stories from subcategories, such as NFL, NBA, MLB, and Golf.

Like any good newspaper — electronic or otherwise — USA Today also includes the latest sports scores. Scores are updated in real time, and start times are listed for games that haven't begun yet. There are scores for football, baseball, hockey, college football, and college basketball — but fans of World Cup Soccer or the Tour de France will have to find updates on their favorite teams and athletes elsewhere.

Selecting the Weather tab displays your current local weather, including hourly and five-day forecasts. You can also view local and national weather maps. You can even add additional locations if you want to see what the weather is like where you'd rather be. I sometimes check the weather in Santa Barbara just to torture myself.

The Pictures tab displays a selection of current images from a variety of categories, such as sports, celebrities, and science. Pictures are shown full-screen, and you can pivot your device to see the images in landscape mode. Tap a full-screen image and a photo caption appears.

Lastly, the Snapshots tab includes USA Today's famous Snapshots infographics, which provide interesting tidbits of information about a wide variety of subject matters. Scroll left or right to see different Snapshots, and you can even cast your vote in a poll on a related topic. I voted yes in the poll that appears in the figure on the right.

Best features

Even when your Android device is offline, you can still read all of the news stories in full, as of the last time USA Today updated its contents.

Worst features

USA Today doesn't necessarily offer the most in-depth news stories, so its light content isn't going to suit everyone's taste. If you want to read "meatier" news stories, some other free news apps that might better wet your whistle are BBC News, NYTimes, and NPR News (which I discuss earlier in this chapter).

WeatherBug Elite
$1.99 US

It never ceases to amaze me how many people get caught in the rain without umbrellas. But then I remember that not everyone checks the weather on his or her Android device before heading out the door, like I do. Some Android handsets, like the models from HTC, come with a widget on the home screen that displays the current weather. Of course, knowing the current temperature and conditions won't necessarily prepare you for the thunderstorm that's supposed to hit in the early evening — or what's due to blow in for the rest of the week.

That's where a dedicated weather app like WeatherBug Elite comes in awfully handy. In addition to the current conditions, it gives an extended forecast up to seven days out. WeatherBug Elite breaks the weather outlook down to morning and evening forecasts, and even provides hourly forecasts that include data such as humidity, wind speed, and chance of precipitation. Of course, as with any weather forecast, the further out the forecast prognosticates, the less accurate it's likely to be.

By default, WeatherBug Elite is set to discover your current location and display the forecast for that local area. You can add additional locations for WeatherBug Elite to monitor — which is especially helpful if you are a frequent traveler. You can also set it to display severe weather alert notifications, which I found particularly valuable when there was a tornado warning in my area recently.

One of my favorite features of WeatherBug Elite is its animated radar map. Choose from a number of map layers to view, such as Radar, U.S. Satellite, and Humidity. You can see an example of the Radar map in the figure on the right. WeatherBug Elite includes a few additional map layers that the free version of the app (WeatherBug) doesn't include, such as Wind Speed and Pressure. The main difference between WeatherBug Elite and WeatherBug, however, is that WeatherBug includes ads, while WeatherBug Elite is completely ad-free.

Sometime you've got to see it to believe it, and WeatherBug Elite lets you do just that with its live camera feeds. Not every area has live cameras, but if you live in a reasonably populated area, there's a good chance there are at least a few live camera feeds available — frequently these feeds come from cameras mounted on the roofs of schools.

Other nifty features are a U.S. pollen count map and a daily national weather forecast video. You can also set WeatherBug Elite to place an icon with the current temperature in your device's status bar notifications area. You can set how frequently this is updated, with options that range from every 15 minutes to once every six hours. You can even set WeatherBug Elite to automatically disable this feature when your device's battery gets below a level that you specify.

I'd be remiss if I didn't mention that there are possibly more weather apps in the Android Market than any other type of app. At least it feels that way. Many of these are excellent apps, such as The Weather Channel app that I discuss later in this chapter. But what makes WeatherBug Elite stand out amongst its peers are the level of detail it provides and the ease with which you can find everything.

Best features

Real-time weather alerts when the weather takes a turn for the worse.

Worst features

It would be great if the video forecast updated more frequently than just once per day.

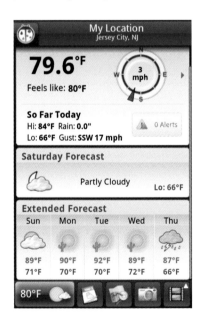

AP Mobile
Free

Yes, AP Mobile is yet another news app; but it has a number of things going for it that most other news apps lack. First and foremost, the Associated Press (AP) gets its news from more than 1,200 sources around the world, which makes AP Mobile an excellent source for international news coverage. AP Mobile has a lot of settings — some might argue an overwhelming number of settings — for exactly what kinds of news stories you want it to display. Last, but not least, AP Mobile includes a collection of 20 photos and 20 videos of the day's news. My only gripe with AP Mobile is that I wish the videos were higher quality.

 ## Earthquake!
Free

Did you feel that? Was that an earthquake? If you think you just felt the earth move under your feet, fire up Earthquake! and you'll quickly find out if there really was one, what its magnitude was, and how close you are to the epicenter. Using data piped in from the U.S. Geological Survey, Earthquake! displays a list of recent earthquakes from around the world. It also has a cool map view that displays an earthquake's epicenter, magnitude, estimated damage zone, and approximate rumble zone (how far out the shaking can be felt). If you live near a quake-prone zone, you can even set Earthquake! to alert you when nearby earthquakes strike. Clean underwear is not included.

 ## Hurricane Hub
Free

Whether you live in harm's way or you consider yourself a virtual storm chaser, Hurricane Hub dishes out the latest Hurricane updates and information. Hurricane Hub offers info about how to prepare for a storm and deal with its aftermath. It also delivers the latest hurricane-related news and provides related information, such as what the different storm categories mean. Perhaps the most interesting feature is the app's different storm maps, which include computer models and five-day storm track predictions. There's even a feature that lets users upload storm photos. When I looked at Hurricane Hub, it was a relatively new app and still a bit rough around the edges; but it already offers enough to make it a worthwhile download, with the promise of improvements down the road.

NewsRob

Free (ad supported)

If you use Google Reader on your computer to aggregate news stories from multiple sources, then NewsRob should be your first choice for accessing those feeds from your Android device. NewsRob automatically syncs with Google Reader, pulling your feeds down to your device so that you can read the content even when it's offline. NewsRob has an elegant, easy-to-use interface, and you can even set NewsRob to notify you when particular feeds are updated. Perhaps the one failing of NewsRob is that you can't use it to subscribe to new feeds — that has to be done directly on the Google Reader Web site. There is also a €4.99 version (NewsRob Pro), which doesn't have ads and which adds a few more features.

The Weather Channel

Free (ad supported)

I'm a big fan of WeatherBug (which I discuss earlier in this chapter), but The Weather Channel comes in a very close second as a worthy weather app. They have a lot in common: They can both track the weather of multiple locations, offer hourly and extended forecasts, and display animated weather maps with multiple layer options. The Weather Channel shows forecasts out to ten days (as opposed to WeatherBug's seven days) and includes a local video forecast that is updated throughout the day. (WeatherBug only has a daily national weather video forecast.) I prefer WeatherBug because of its severe weather alerts and the more detailed weather information it provides.

11 Photography and Video

Top Ten Apps

- Adobe Photoshop Express
- Camera360 Ultimate
- Foxy Photo Editor
- Ustream Broadcaster
- Vignette
- CamCalc Free
- OrbLive
- Photobucket Mobile
- Photofluent
- Time-Lapse

Adobe Photoshop Express
Free

When it comes to editing digital images, the first name that typically comes to mind is Adobe Photoshop. Many professional photographers rely on the application's powerful image-manipulation features, and so do many photography enthusiasts and even less-serious-minded users who want to touch up images or experiment with different effects. For a price, Photoshop is available in a number of incarnations for Windows and Mac computers; but with the free Adobe Photoshop Express app, your Android device can get in on the image-editing action too.

It's a given that Adobe Photoshop Express doesn't have anywhere near as many bells and whistles as the computer-based versions of Photoshop do, but it still packs a wallop in terms of what it can do to make the photos you shoot with your device's camera look better.

When you launch Adobe Photoshop Express, the first screen displays thumbnails of all the image files stored on your device's SD card. At the bottom of the screen are Edit and Upload buttons. Tap the Edit button and then the image you want to edit to launch the image editor. Tap the Upload button, choose whether you want to upload to a Photoshop.com account (up to 2GB of free online storage), a Facebook account, or post an image to Twitter using a free Twitpic account, and then choose the image to upload.

 If you have a Photoshop.com account, you can configure Adobe Photoshop Express to automatically upload any new pictures you shoot with your device's camera. Note that this does *not* include images you edit with Adobe Photoshop Express and then save to your device — those you have to upload manually.

Adobe Photoshop Express has four sets of editing tools. The first one lets you Crop, Straighten, Rotate, and Flip the image. The Crop tool includes the capability to crop to 1:1, 3:4, and 4:3 aspect ratios if you so choose.

The second set of tools includes the image adjustment tools, which you can see in the figure below. With the exception of Black & White, after you a select a tool, you adjust the tool's strength by sliding your finger across the image. When you like what you see, tap the green check mark. If you decide you don't want to implement the change, tap the red X.

The third tool is the Soft Focus tool, which you also control by sliding your finger across the image. The last set of tools includes the Effects and Borders tools. Choose from a total of seven effects and eight borders. When you select an Effect or Border, you see a preview of what the image will look like before you accept the change.

Best features

If you make any mistakes along the way, Adobe Photoshop Express includes multiple levels of undo and redo. Also, when you save an image, Adobe Photoshop Express saves the edited image as a new file, leaving the original image file untouched.

Worst features

Although you can upload images to a Photoshop.com account, you can't download them from a Photoshop.com account to your device.

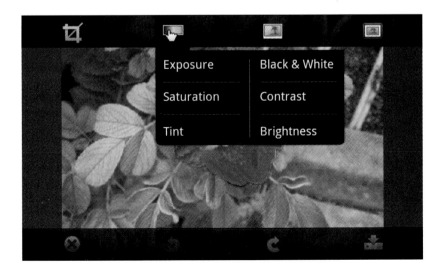

Camera360 Ultimate
$3.99 US

As the reviews in this chapter attest, there are oodles of camera apps available for Android devices. Nearly all of them add features to the mix that most Android devices' default camera apps don't typically offer. Camera360 Ultimate is one of my favorite camera apps because it includes some of my all-time favorite effects. And like Vignette (which I also review in this chapter), Camera360 Ultimate applies its effects to your pictures *as you shoot them.*

Following are just some of Camera360 Ultimate's effects that can create truly eye-popping images:

- **HDR simulation (Heavy):** This effect simulates an image that's captured using high dynamic range (HDR) photography, where a wider than normal range of light and dark areas of an image are captured. Photos shot with this mode tend to have oversaturated colors and high contrast, which results in images that have an artistic feel to them.

- **Back to 1839:** Photos shot with this effect look like they were shot more than 170 years ago. Images are black and white and very grainy. Stains and scratches give them that been-around-for-a-bunch-of-decades look.

- **Surrealist Color Painting:** In my opinion, this effect is mislabeled. I don't think photos captured with this effect look anything like surrealist paintings—impressionist paintings maybe, but not surrealist. But that doesn't stop me from enjoying the way photos look with this effect—which to me is more like a sketch done with soft pastels. This is the effect that was used in the figure below.

- **Line Sketch:** This effect is very similar to the Surrealist Color Painting, but instead of color pastels, the image looks like it was drawn in pencil.

- **Four-colour Poster:** This effect results in a picture that reproduces the image four times in a square grid. Each of the four squares is a different monochromatic color and has very high contrast, making it look like it was silkscreened. The concept here is to make an image that is reminiscent of something that Andy Warhol might have created.

✔ **Colour-shift Mode:** This ingenious effect has you first select an
area of an image that you are about to shoot. The resulting photograph is black and white, except for any parts of the image that
are the same color as the area you selected. Imagine a photo of a
giraffe with orange spots, but everything else is black and white,
and you get an idea of what this effect does. You can also set
this effect to do the opposite, where it removes only the selected
color from the image.

Even without all these effects, Camera360 Ultimate is a full-featured
camera app. It has a wide range of resolution and compression quality settings, includes a number of white balance settings, has a timer
option, supports geotagging, and even includes image-stabilization
features.

Best features

After you shoot a picture, a preview window opens, showing the
resulting image. If you used an effect, tap and hold the image to see
what the picture looks like without the effect (this works for most, but
not all the effects). You can also set Camera360 Ultimate to automatically save "unedited" versions of images shot using effects.

Worst features

Camera360 Ultimate includes a mode that is meant to emulate tilt-shift
photography, which makes real scenes look like they're actually shots
of miniatures. No matter how much I tried, I couldn't get this mode to
create a decent-looking image.

Foxy Photo Editor
€1.99

Foxy Photo Editor is quite simply the most powerful image editor I've come across for Android devices. A good number of its features are of an advanced-enough nature that they are more commonly found in pricey image editing software that runs on desktop computers. If you want to use your Android device to touch up your photos, Foxy Photo Editor will most assuredly get the job done.

Foxy Photo Editor breaks out its image editing capabilities into five sections: Access the Transform and Filters selections from the device's Menu button, and use the Tools button on the screen to access the Paint, Photo Edit, and Draw tools.

The most rudimentary of Foxy Photo Editor's features are its Transform tools, which modify an entire image by enabling you to do things like Crop, Rotate, or Flip an image.

Foxy Photo Editor's Filters also apply wholesale alterations to an image, changing attributes such as its Brightness and Contrast, Hue and Saturation, and Color balance. You can also alter an image's over-all appearance with the Dodge, Blur, or Shrink filters. There are even filters that give you more creative license, such as Posterize, Oilify, and Color noise. Many of these filters have sliders that you move across the screen with your finger to set the strength that the filter applies to the image.

 Whenever you apply a Filter, you accept the change by tapping the green check mark, or reject the change by tapping the red X. While there is no undo feature that lets you completely undo the filter you just applied, Foxy Photo Editor includes a nifty Undo brush tool that allows you to selectively undo *portions* of the filter you just used. For instance, if you apply the Grayscale filter to an image, you can use the Undo brush tool to bring back the color to portions of the image.

The Paint tool includes an assortment of brushes, such as Finger paint, Paintbrush, and Airbrush, which you can use to paint on top of an image, or even create a new image from scratch. After you select a brush, tap the Color Chooser button to pick the color the brush will paint with. Tap and hold one of the color swatches to edit the color. As you can see in the figure on the left, you can set a color's Hue,

Saturation, Value, and Transparency — all the while seeing a preview of what the edited color looks like. Next, tap the Brush Options button to select a brush tip style, and then set the brush's Size and Exposure.

The Draw tool provides a handful of basic options, such as basic shapes, text balloons, text, and clip art. Each of these tools includes many options for size, proportions, and colors. The text tools offer an array of fonts to pick from.

Best features

The most robust part of Foxy Photo Editor is its Photo Edit tools. In addition to the ones that appear in the figure on the right, other Photo Edit tools include Warp, Pixelize, and Blur. These are the key tools for modifying select portions of the image. With these tools, you use the Brush Options to set the size and strength of the tools.

Worst features

Regardless of how high the resolution of your source image is, Foxy Photo Editor is limited to editing images that are no larger than 1,024 x 768 (or a resolution with the equivalent number of total pixels). If you try to open a larger image, the app states that it is too large to be edited and gives you the option of automatically resizing it for editing.

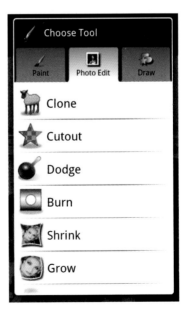

Ustream Broadcaster
Free

A famous song from the 1970s said that "The Revolution Will Not Be Televised." No, instead it will be streamed live over the Internet. And with Ustream Broadcaster, it could very well be streamed live from an Android device.

While you're waiting for the revolution (be it cultural, technological, or otherwise), you can use Ustream Broadcaster to send a live video and audio broadcast of practically any event — be it a graduation, wedding, or your kid's kindergarten puppet show. Broadcasting this sort of life event over the Internet is what has come to be called "lifecasting." But what you broadcast need not be so personal. You could tap dance, host your own talk show, or send out a live feed of your ant farm.

Starting a live stream couldn't be simpler. Just launch Ustream Broadcaster and tap the Live button. Assuming you've already created an account and previously entered your log-in credentials, the very next screen displayed will be what your device's camera sees. Tap the Go Live button and you're broadcasting. That's it. From launching the app to streaming live can happen in as little as ten seconds. That is, of course, assuming that your device has an active Wi-Fi or 3G connection.

If you're using Ustream Broadcaster, chances are you want someone to watch what you're streaming. You can set Ustream Broadcaster to automatically send out a Tweet announcing that you're now broadcasting, and it will include a link to where your fans can watch the stream on the Ustream Web site (www.ustream.tv).

Users watching your broadcast from the Ustream site can send out a chat message that appears on the screen of everyone who's watching your broadcast. You can see such a message in the figure below. While you're broadcasting, Ustream Broadcaster also shows you how long you've been live for and how many viewers you have. You can also initiate a simple Yes/No poll and see the results onscreen as your viewers cast their votes.

 The settings in Ustream Broadcaster are pretty basic. If you want more control over how your broadcasts look and who can see them, you need to configure your account settings on the Ustream site. There you can do things like create multiple broadcast shows, turn off the chat feature, and mark your shows as private so only those viewers who know the password can watch it. By default, all of your shows are available for anyone to watch.

When you finish broadcasting, Ustream Broadcaster gives you the options of saving the video to your device and uploading it to the Ustream site and your YouTube account. You can have Ustream Broadcaster send out links to your uploaded video from your Twitter and Facebook accounts. You can also use Ustream Broadcaster to record a video offline and then upload it later.

Best features

With a speedy data connection, the video and audio quality are pretty decent. Your viewers might not realize that you're broadcasting from an Android device.

Worst features

Even if you're lucky enough to have an Android device that has a forward-facing camera, it isn't going to do you much good here. Ustream Broadcaster won't support it. Ustream Broadcaster only works with the primary cameras, typically located on the *back* of Android devices.

Qik is a similar broadcasting app for Android devices, and it works with forward-facing cameras. I've had lots of problems getting Qik to work right, so at least for me, Ustream Broadcaster is a much more reliable app.

**Vignette**
£2.49

There's a good reason why Vignette is one of the most popular Android camera apps. With more than 70 effects and 50 frame styles to choose from, Vignette offers more options to enhance your photos than practically any other camera app. (Each effect also includes over 20 custom settings for even further adjustments.) And like Camera360 Ultimate, Vignette applies the effects when you shoot your pictures. Vignette can also add frames to the pictures you shoot — which is something Camera360 Ultimate can't do.

You can see a small sampling of Vignette's many effects in the figure on the left. The entries that have down-facing arrows next to them, such as Toy Camera, are actually category headings that expand into lists of related effects. For instance, some of the Vintage effects include Faded, Summer, and Yearbook. The additional effects categories that you can't see in the figure are Tinted monochrome, Lens Effects, Cinematic, and Miscellaneous. If you feel adventurous, set any of the effects categories to Random to get a photographic surprise every time you press the shutter.

The available frames include bordered, rounded, black, and oval shapes for a number of different images sizes and aspect ratios. Some of the odder frame type categories include Grungy and Film effect. You can also set Vignette to apply a random frame to your shots. If you frequently use particular combinations of effects and frames, you can save them as favorites.

The figure on the right shows what Vignette's screen looks like when it's in camera mode. The dark border around the image indicates where the frame type you've selected will overlay over the image. Vignette can geotag your photos, and the Location accuracy message at the top of the screen tells you how accurate the geotagging of the image will be. If you tap the No zoom button in the upper-right corner of the screen, you can choose to use a software-based zoom (also known as digital zoom) to expand a portion of the image, or you can choose to crop part of the image.

The information at the bottom of the screen tells you the different settings that currently are in place. From left to right, these are settings for Shooting mode, Flash mode, Camera hardware settings, JPEG file settings, and Effects and Frame. Some of the possible shooting modes are Steady shot, Self timer, and Time Lapse. You set the flash to off, auto, or on. The camera hardware settings include things such as setting the Scene mode, White balance, and Focus distance. The JPEG file settings let you set things like Resolution, Quality, and in which folder images are saved.

You can also apply any of Vignette's effects and frame styles to images that are already saved to your device's memory. Tap your device's Menu button, and then tap the Import button to see all the images that are saved to your device's memory — even those images that were initially saved by Vignette. (Next to the Import button is a Gallery button, which displays thumbnails of all the images that Vignette has saved. You'd think that you could load images into Vignette from the Gallery screen, but you'd be wrong. All you can do on the Gallery screen is delete images or share them.)

Best features

If you enable the Save originals setting, Vignette will save two versions of each photograph it takes — one with the effects and frames applied to it and one without any effects or frames.

Worst features

There is no way to preview what your pictures will look like ahead of time. What appears on the screen in camera mode doesn't change when you adjust the effects settings.

CamCalc Free
Free (ad supported)

If your photographic endeavors involve more than just pointing and shooting, you need a photography calculator to help you get the perfect shot. CamCalc includes eight calculators for use with still cameras (film and digital), video cameras, and even motion-picture cameras. The included calculators are Depth of Field, Field of View, Focal Length Equivalents, Flash Calculations, Color Temp. Conversion, Miniatures, Solar Calculations (sunrise and sunset times), and Exposure Compensation. For each calculator, just input the variables (such as camera format, focal length, and f-stop for depth of field), and CamCalc displays the relevant data. For $1.99, you can get a version of CamCalc that doesn't include ads, and with which the location-aware Solar Calculations calculator also displays a graph of the sun path for the day.

OrbLive
$9.99 US

OrbLive lets you watch video and photo files and listen to music files that are sitting back at home on your computer. And if your computer has a TV tuner, you can even use OrbLive to watch live TV on your Android device. OrbLive works anywhere that your device has a Wi-Fi, Edge, 3G, or 4G signal; faster connections mean sharper looking images and better sounding audio.

In order for OrbLive to do this, you need to install the free Orb Caster software on your computer (downloadable from `www.orb.com`) and leave your computer running. Your computer also needs to be reasonably speedy so that it can perform the conversion of your media files for streaming to your device. Unfortunately, this process can be persnickety at times and there might be all sorts of compatibility issues with some of your media files, computer, network connection, or Android device. So before you plunk down ten bucks for the app, take the free OrbLive Free app for an extended spin to make sure everything works the way you want it to.

Photobucket Mobile
Free (ad supported)

What good is a photograph if you can't share it with other people? Photobucket Mobile makes it super-easy to share pictures you shot using your Android device. You need a free Photobucket account (which you can sign up for within the app or at `www.photobucket.com`), but after it's set up, you can upload photos and videos to your online Photobucket albums. You can even set Photobucket Mobile to automatically upload all new photos you take with your device. You can also view and manage your online albums, download photos, and send out links to your photos.

With a free Photobucket account, you can only store up to 500MB worth of photos. Purchase a Photobucket Pro account ($2.99 per month) for unlimited storage.

Photofluent
Free

Photofluent doesn't take pictures, but it will help you capture better-looking photographs by providing lots of valuable information and tips. Geared toward amateur photographers, Photofluent provides scads of details for a wide variety of indoor (such as sports and weddings), outdoor (such as fireworks and kids), and special-situation (such as panoramas and high dynamic range) photography. Each article indicates whether the concept is for beginners, intermediates, or experts, and includes an example image, sample camera settings, details, and suggestions.

Time-Lapse
$1.99 US

Time-Lapse is a fun app for making your own time-lapse movies — the movies where you watch flowers bloom in seconds or traffic whiz by at unrealistic speeds. You can create videos at resolutions that range from 176 x 144 up to whatever the maximum resolution of your device's camera is (in the case of my Samsung Epic 4G, it's a whopping 2,560 x 1,920). You can set Time-Lapse to automatically capture images at rates from once per second up to one frame every 60 minutes. You can also set the playback rate of the recorded video to anywhere between 1 frame per second (fps) and 30 fps.

After you record a video, you can watch it using the Time-Lapse app, upload it to YouTube, or e-mail it. But note that Time-Lapse records video in a format that most Windows or Mac video playback software does not support. So your best bet for viewing these videos on a computer is to do so using the free VLC media player (which you can download at `www.videolan.org`).

12 Productivity and Business

Documents To Go
$29.99 US

I don't think the smartphone is going to replace the laptop anytime soon as the primary portable device people use for productivity tasks. Still, with the right app installed, there's certainly no reason why you *can't* use a smartphone to do many of the things you can do on a laptop. For instance, with Documents To Go, you can work with Microsoft Word, Excel, and PowerPoint files directly on your Android device.

And when I say "work," I don't mean you can just read them. You can create, edit, and format doc, docx, xls, xlsx, ppt, and pptx files. You can also read PDF files, sync your documents with your Windows PC, and even read and edit your Google Docs documents. If you're used to using any of the Microsoft Office apps or Google Docs, you should feel right at home with Documents To Go.

The figure on left shows Documents To Go's main screen. To open documents stored on your device, select the Local Files tab, which then opens a file browser screen from which you can navigate to the document you wish to open. On the file browser screen, you can view file properties, delete files, and assign a star to a file to make it easier to locate later. From the main screen, you can access recently opened documents and starred files, as well as access documents stored online from your Google Docs account. Here you can also create new Word, Excel, or PowerPoint documents (via the "+" button on the bottom of the screen), and select which files to sync with your desktop PC (which requires installing a free app on your computer, downloadable from www.dataviz.com).

With Word documents, you have a wide variety of text formatting options to choose from, such as picking different fonts and font attributes, paragraph formatting, bullets and numbering, and adding bookmarks. You can also insert page breaks, tables, and comments. When editing, you can select, cut, copy, paste, undo, and redo.

You don't have quite as many formatting options with Excel documents as you do with Word documents, but you still have a lot of control over how individual cells look. (See the figure on the right.) You can insert rows, columns, worksheets, and functions — Documents To Go includes a whopping 111 Excel functions.

With PowerPoint documents, you have even fewer formatting options. As far as document creation or editing, you can do little more than add text (with no font options), add bullet items, increase and decrease indents, and arrange slide order. That said, you can still use Documents To Go to view PowerPoint documents that have elaborate formatting with static images.

Best features

With Documents To Go, it's like having a lite version of the Microsoft Office suite installed on your Android device.

Worst features

Documents To Go is an expensive app, so unless you require frequent mobile access to your Microsoft Office documents, the cost might not be justifiable.

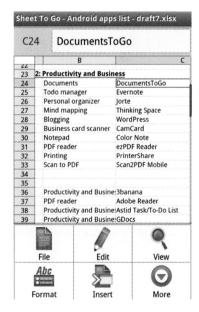

Evernote
Free

I freely admit that I'm one of *those* people who keep lots of lists. I've got my ever-changing to-do list, the car maintenance schedule, a growing list of books I want to read, and that's just to name a few. I have many things I want to keep track of and remember, but there simply isn't enough room in my brain to manage it at all. Thankfully, with Evernote, I don't have to.

Actually, Evernote is much more than just a list manager. In addition to typing the information you want to remember, you can capture images using your device's camera and audio notes using your device's microphone. You can also attach PDF, photo, audio, and video files to notes. Notes can even have multiple files attached to them. You can add tags to your notes and search through your notes for specific words.

Where Evernote truly shines, however, is in its capability to sync your notes to the Evernote online service, which then enables you to access your notes from virtually any other mobile device or computer: You can easily access your notes on the Evernote Web site (`www.evernote.com`) using a Web browser. Evernote has free desktop applications you can install on Windows and Mac PCs, and free versions for iPhones, iPads, iPod touches, BlackBerry devices, Windows Mobile devices, and Palm Pre and Palm Pixi devices.

 If you use Evernote on more than one device and want to access all of your notes during those instances when your device doesn't have an Internet connection, consider subscribing to Evernote's Premium service ($5 per month or $45 per year). With a Premium subscription, Evernote stores local copies of all of your notes on your devices whenever it syncs. Otherwise, when your device is offline and you're using the free version of the Evernote service, you can access only notes created on *that* device. You can see some notes that were created on other devices, but *only* if you've previously opened these notes — and even then, you'll only see what was in the note as of the last time you read it, not the last time you synced your notes.

A Premium subscription offers other additional benefits, such as larger storage space with the Evernote service and support for larger note sizes. With a premium subscription, you can also attach any file type to a note.

Best features

When you add a photo to a note, Evernote automatically scans it to see if it contains any recognizable text. If it finds text, Evernote adds the text to its index. This means that when you search for text within your notes, Evernote will include the photos in its search results that contain the text you are searching for. For instance, if you have a photo of a stop sign in your notes and you search for the text "stop," the photo of the stop sign should appear in your search results.

If you subscribe to the Evernote premium service, recognizable text within PDF files will also appear in search results.

Worst features

It's a shame that when you're offline you can't easily access all of your notes — regardless of which device they were created on — without paying for a premium subscription.

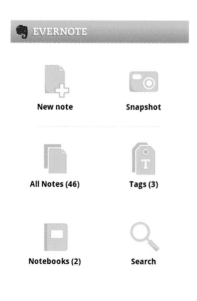

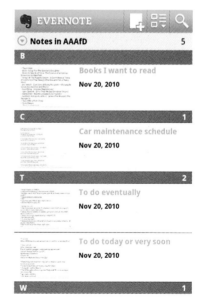

Jorte
Free

Many folks tell you that you must control your own destiny, but they often neglect to tell you how. I don't claim to have the answer to this quandary, but I do know that the first step is to organize all your appointments, tasks, and to-do's into an appointment book, calendar, or personal organizer. And of all the Android apps that serve this purpose, my favorite is Jorte.

Use Jorte as a stand-alone calendar or sync it with your Google Calendar. If your device already syncs with your Google Calendar, you don't need to change any settings — Jorte automatically accesses your settings. If your device doesn't yet sync with your Google Calendar and you want Jorte to access it, go into your device's settings (not Jorte's settings) to enable Google Calendar synchronization. If you need help figuring out how to do this, check out the handy instructions at `jorte.net/english/synchro.html`. While you're at the Jorte Web site, peruse some of the other pages there for additional tips on configuring and using the app.

Jorte includes a boatload of settings for how it appears. Pick from a number of multicolored display styles, such as Jorte White (which is what you see in the figure on the left), Sky Blue, or Strawberry Milk. Change the fonts for different sections of the calendar, such as the month name, day number, and text with calendar entries — you can even download additional fonts. You can also select which day you want the different views to start on — for instance, you can have the monthly view start on a Sunday, but set the weekly view to start on a Monday.

Speaking of views, there are a plethora to choose from, including three different types of weekly views, a 14-day view, and a horizontal view. If you subscribe to multiple Google Calendars, you can specify which of them you want to appear in the calendar. You can set whether you want to see tasks, and you can even use separate Google Calendars for your calendar and your tasks. You can set your tasks to appear on the bottom of the display, and you can choose to have your tasks appear in the calendar as well.

When viewing the calendar, tap on a date to see a list of all the events that are scheduled for that day. Below the list of the day's events are options to enter a new event, view the preceding day, or see the next day (see the figure on the right). If you tap an existing event, a screen pops up with all the details about that event, plus options to delete it, copy it, edit it, or mark it as completed.

When you enter a new event, you have the option of choosing an existing event from the event history. If you do this, it copies all of the information from the previous event, and then you can just edit those aspects that are different for this new event, such as the date and time. Other data you can provide for an event are its location, a description, recurring information, and multiple reminders.

Best features

With its many configuration options and varied views to choose from, you can set Jorte exactly how you want it to look and work.

Worst features

You can't enter new tasks by selecting a date on the calendar, like you can with new events. To enter a new task, you must select Tasks and Memo from the menu, and then tap the New Tasks & Memo button.

Thinking Space Pro
£2.39

Before I dive into Thinking Space Pro, I first need to explain what mind mapping is . . . When you plan a task or project or brainstorm an idea, a simple list sometimes isn't enough. The problem with lists is that they are linear and are not well suited for connected ideas that share complex relationships. A mind map, however, is inherently nonlinear and is built entirely on related concepts that branch off into further related concepts. Pardon the pun, but a mind map actually encourages you to *be all over the map* as you explore an idea.

The result is a graphical diagram of interrelated items that represents a holistic view of a task, project, or idea. Think of a mind map as a project's "org chart." The figure on the left shows an example of what a Thinking Space Pro mind map looks like.

Each item in a mind map is basically just a piece of text, called a node. You can build a mind map by adding more nodes and creating relationships between the different nodes.

To start building a mind map, select New MindMap from the app's main screen. Then give the mind map a name, which also becomes the mind map's title node. With the title node selected, tap the green plus-sign (+) icon in the toolbar on the bottom of the screen to create a new connected node. To make additional connections, first select the node you want to connect to, and then add a new node.

By default, all the nodes will look similar, so once your mind map starts filling up, change the way your nodes look. Double-tap a node to open a toolbar with three buttons: Text, Node, and Tools. Tap the Text button to open the Text toolbar, which lets you set the node's text style, size, and color. You can also add a text note to a node.

Tap the Node button to open the Node Toolbar, which lets you set that node's graphics' style and color. You can also add icons and hyperlinks to a node. A hyperlink creates an association between a node and any file stored on your device, such as a photo or video file, or even another Thinking Space Pro mind map file.

Tap the Tools button to open the Tools Toolbar, which lets you arrange the order that nodes appear and create an additional connection between two nodes, whether they are already connected or not. Thinking Space Pro calls this type of connection a "relation," and the figure on the left shows an example of this with the connection between the Uses node and the Tips node.

To share a mind map, export it as a PNG, text, or MindManager file. Thinking Space Pro also includes a "cloud" feature that lets you sync your mind maps with online storage (which requires installing an additional free plug-in). If you sync your maps using the cloud feature, you can share your maps with other users and let them make changes to the maps. The updated maps are then synced back to your device.

Mind mapping isn't for everyone, but if you'd like to give it a shot without first making a financial investment, install the free, advertising-supported version of Thinking Space.

Best features

Thinking Space Pro comes with a bunch of useful gestures that make adding and editing nodes a breeze. You can see some of the available gestures in the figure on the right, which is from the detailed Help screen.

Worst features

If you aren't familiar with mind mapping, getting up to speed with Thinking Space Pro can be a steep learning curve.

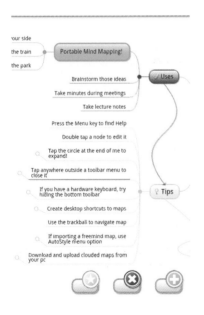

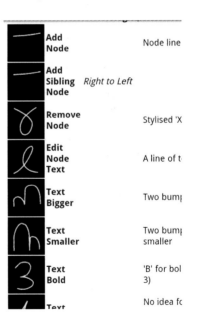

WordPress
Free

On the Internet, it seems like everybody's got something to say and someplace to say it. For many, the soapbox of choice is a personal blog, where they get to share everything from their political opinions to thoughts about what color socks to wear. While there are numerous ways to blog, the most popular blogging tool is WordPress; if you are a WordPress user (or want to be), you can use the WordPress Android app to post, edit, and manage your blogs while on the go.

 The WordPress Android app works with blogs hosted on `wordpress.com`, as well as with self-hosted WordPress blogs. The WordPress app can manage multiple WordPress blogs.

The top of the screen for each blog you manage includes four buttons:

- ✔ **Comments:** This opens the Comments screen, where you can see all the recent comments that readers have left on your blog. Tap an entry to see the full text of the comment as well as options to delete it, reply, mark it as spam, and approve or unapprove the comment. Tapping the Edit button in the lower-left corner of the Comments screen opens check boxes next to each comment entry, which lets you delete, mark as spam, unapprove, or approve multiple comments at the same time (see the figure on the left).

- ✔ **Posts:** This opens the Posts screen, where you manage your existing blog posts and create new posts. Tap an existing blog post and a screen pops up with options to view the post, view comments, edit the post, and delete it.

  Tap the plus sign in the lower-left corner of the Posts screen (see the figure on the right) to open the New Post screen. Here you can give your new post a title, add content, add media, and assign tags and categories. Text-formatting options are bold, italic, underline, strikethrough, add a link, and insert block quotes. You can save your drafts to your device, upload drafts to your blog, and publish your post.

✔ **Pages:** This opens the Pages screen, where you manage any of your blog's pages, such as About and Contact pages, or add new pages. Tap an entry for an existing page to view the page, see comments, edit the page, or delete it.

✔ **Stats:** This opens the Stats screen, where you can see statistics for your blog for things like views, search terms, and clicks. Select to see data from anywhere between the last 7 days and for as long as the blog has existed.

Best features

For each blog you manage, you can set the WordPress app to notify you whenever someone posts a comment. You can set the update interval to between every 5 minutes and once per day.

Worst features

The app doesn't have as many formatting options as you get when you use the online `wordpress.com` blogging tool. For instance, with the WordPress Android app, you can't add photo captions, align text, or check spelling.

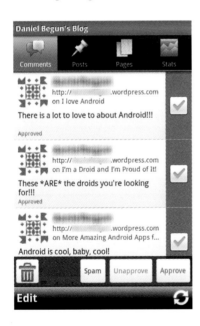

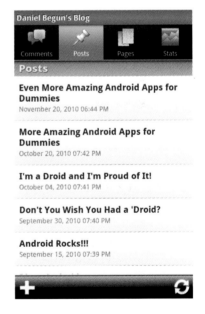

CamCard
$6.99 US

It used to be that whenever someone handed me a business card, I made a mental note to enter the information into my contacts as soon as I got a chance. Nine times out of ten, that chance never came and the business card wound up in a growing pile of cards I planned to get to some day. Now, whenever someone hands me a business card, I whip out my phone, fire up CamCard, and take a picture of the card. Within a few seconds, CamCard scans the image using optical character recognition (OCR) technology and extracts all the relevant information, such as the person's name and title, company name, address, phone number, e-mail address, and Web site. I quickly review the information, make any necessary corrections, and save it to my phone's contacts or my Google contacts. Now that's what I call productivity!

ColorNote Notepad Notes
Free

I'm not quite sure I understand the need for the redundancy in the name of the ColorNote Notepad Notes app, but I do get that it's a powerful notepad app. Notes are entered either as simple text notes or line-by-line checklists. In addition to giving each note a title, you can assign one of nine colors to each note. You can also password-protect your notes and back them up to your SD Card. When an item in a checklist is done, check it off as completed. Although ColorNote Notepad Notes doesn't have anywhere near the breadth of features that Evernote does (reviewed earlier in this chapter), ColorNote Notepad Notes has one very useful feature that Evernote lacks, and that is the capability to assign reminders to your notes.

ezPDF Reader
$0.99 US

Plenty of PDF readers are available for Android devices, and a number of them are free. But ezPDF is by far the best of the bunch and well worth its 99-cent price tag, because it lets you adjust how the PDF files appear on the screen. For instance, the Text Reflow mode reflows the text of pages that are difficult to read pages into an easier to read format. When using this feature, you can also opt to use Night

Mode, which displays the document as white text against a black background. Another awesome feature is that you can search for text within a PDF, and ezPDF will inform you how many times it appears and even highlight each occurrence. Another thing ezPDF does is let you select text within a document, copy it to the clipboard, paste it into another app, or do a search for the selected text on the Web.

PrinterShare Premium
$4.95 US

PrinterShare lets Android devices do something that they aren't designed to do: print. With PrinterShare installed, your device can print pictures, Web pages, calendar events, contacts, e-mail messages, call logs, Google Docs, and PDF files to nearby Wi-Fi and Bluetooth-enabled printers. PrinterShare can also print to a printer that's connected to a computer that's running the Bonjour service (which is built into the Mac OS and available for Windows PC for free from support.apple.com/kb/DL999).

Even better, you can send a print job from your device to nearly any printer — no matter where in the world it is — as long as the printer is connected to a system that's running the free PrinterShare software (www.printershare.com/download-windows.sdf).

PrinterShare doesn't work with every printer or Android device, so there's no guarantee that it will work with your particular setup. Also note that remote printing requires first creating a PrinterShare account, and you need a paid subscription if you plan on printing more than a handful of printed pages remotely each month.

Scan2PDF Mobile 2.0
£3.99

Scan2PDF Mobile is a simple app that lets you snap a photo of a document, then it automatically converts the image into a PDF file and saves the file to your device's SD Card. You can convert existing photos to PDF files, rotate converted images, create multi-page documents, and send converted files via e-mail. You can also adjust the image quality of the scans and set the PDF page size to A4 or letter size. Use Scan2PDF Mobile in concert with PrinterShare (reviewed earlier in this chapter) and your device acts as a portable photocopy machine!

13 Reference

Google Goggles

Free

To conduct a Web search, you usually type what you are looking for into a text box. (On Android devices, you can also do voice searches, but even your spoken words are automatically turned back into text.) The problem with text searches is that they don't do much good when you don't know what you're looking for, such as when you see something and want to know, "what the heck is that?"

Google Goggles attempts to answer that question. I say "attempts," because the technology is still in its infancy, and its results are anything but reliable at this early stage. Google Goggles uses a nascent technology called "visual search," which looks for matches based on the physical attributes of an object, such as its shape, colors, or unique patterns. Think of it as a fingerprint reader for all the things around you.

Using your device's built-in camera, take a snapshot of the object you wish to identify. Google Goggles analyzes the image and if Google Goggles thinks it knows what the object is, it displays information about the object and provides a list of relevant links.

Google Goggles is good at identifying things that have writing on them, like book covers and product packaging. It's also excellent at reading bar codes and QR codes. (QR Codes are weird-looking, square barcode that have information embedded in them that can be read and interpreted. There's one next to the name Google Goggles above.) Taking this a step further, Google Goggles can scan a business card, turn it into text, and add it to your contacts. You can even have Google Goggles scan something written in a foreign language and translate it into your own native tongue.

But where Google Goggles really shows its potential is in identifying non-text-based objects, like artwork and landmarks. Google Goggles correctly identified every image of well-known artworks I had it scan — such as the one in the figure on the left. In addition to a list of relevant links, the top of the results page identifies the name of the artwork, when it was created, and who the artist was. On the other hand, I didn't have as much luck with *pictures* of landmarks — but Google Goggles does much better with the real thing, where it can also use GPS, therefore knowing *where* the landmark is.

Speaking of GPS, Google Goggles uses your device's GPS and compass to provide information about local businesses. In this instance, text bubbles appear onscreen in front of the business the camera happens to be pointing at. Just tap a bubble and all sorts of information about that business show up on the screen.

You can rate the accuracy of Google Goggles' searches; this feedback helps Google refine its visual search engine. Google Goggles also saves the images you capture, so you can revisit your results later — the figure on the right shows an example of Google Goggles' Search History.

Best features

It's pretty darn amazing to see when Google Goggles accurately identifies an object. But . . .

Worst features

. . . Google Goggles' accuracy in identifying objects still has a long way to go.

Google Sky Map
Free

Google Sky Map will appeal to budding astronomers looking to find their way around the night sky, and in my humble opinion, *anyone* who owns an Android device should install it. Why? Because it's one of the coolest Android apps available!

Here's how Google Sky Map works: You hold your device up to the sky, and the app displays which celestial objects are located in the section of sky directly behind the device. It's as though you were looking straight through your device to see an accurate sky map. Move your device to the left and up, and the view of the sky map moves to the left and up too. It's downright eerie how accurate it can be.

Google Sky Map achieves this level of accuracy by using your device's GPS, compass, and accelerometer. It uses the GPS to get your precise location and time, so make sure you enable your device's GPS. You also must properly calibrate your device's compass. It's easy to do: Just hold your device in front of you and swing it around a couple of times in a figure-eight pattern. You'll look silly, but it works.

Google Sky Map displays stars, constellations, Messier objects, and planets. These all exist as visual layers, which you can toggle on and off. You can also control layers for the right ascension and declination grid, horizon line, and planet images. (If you don't know what these things are, then just count it as one more reason why you should install this app. You'll learn something new!) Planet images appear as small graphics — this helps finding the planets among all the stars much easier. The following figure shows Google Sky Map in landscape mode, with Jupiter, Uranus, and Neptune, all in the same part of the sky. Unfortunately, from my location, none of them were actually visible, as they were all below the horizon (the yellow horizon line running across the top of the screen).

When you're in front of your telescope and need to keep things as dark as possible, Google Sky Map includes a special night mode, which displays all objects in red against a black background (red light has the least adverse affect on night vision). Google Sky Map also includes a cool Time Travel mode that lets you see what the sky looks like at any given point in the past or future.

Best features

Google Sky Map is a Google creation, so you know it has a search built into it. When you search for an object, a ring appears on the screen, with an arrow pointing in the direction of the object. Point your device toward the direction the arrow is pointing and the ring changes color (blue means you are far away, red means you are getting closer). When you finally have the object in sight, the ring turns orange and increases in size to surround the object on the screen. This helps you find objects in the sky, but . . .

Worst features

. . . That's the extent of Google Sky Map's search capabilities. If you tap an object, nothing happens. You don't get information about the object, or even a link to the Web to learn more about it. But because this is a Google creation, I'd be willing to bet that such functionality will eventually make its way into Google Sky Map.

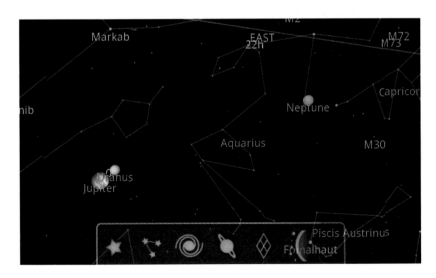

The Merriam-Webster Collegiate Dictionary
$24.95 US

With so many free Android dictionary apps, you might wonder what a $25 dictionary app is doing here. Plenty of free dictionaries are great resources (like Free Dictionary Org, which I discuss in this chapter), but they don't quite measure up to the level of scholarly scrutiny as the Merriam-Webster dictionary and they don't include as many useful features.

There are actually several different versions of the Merriam-Webster English-language dictionary in the Android Market. At the bottom end of the scale is the $14.95 *Merriam-Webster's Pocket Dictionary,* which has 40,000 entries. At the other extreme is the $59.95 *Merriam-Webster's Unabridged Dictionary,* which has more than 257,000 entries. The *Merriam-Webster Collegiate Dictionary*, which I review here, has more than 90,000 entries and 225,000 definitions. There are also free trial versions available in the Android Market.

The number of entries is not the only thing that distinguishes these references from one another. The Pocket Dictionary provides very concise definitions, whereas the Unabridged includes lengthy definitions, usage examples, synonyms, and etymologies. Only academics, spelling bee contestants, and competitive Scrabble players need the Unabridged version. Beyond that, though, the different versions operate the same way and include the same features.

Those features include the capability to look a word up either by typing it or speaking it. Speaking a word has the advantage that as long as you know how to pronounce it, you don't have to know how to spell it. Of course, you must be able to recognize the word you're looking for when the search results come up. The majority of words in the database include easily understood spoken pronunciations, which you can access directly from the word list — such as in the figure on the left.

Tap a word in the list and the definition page for that word opens. In addition to a word's multiple definitions, the page also includes the word's pronunciation, the part of speech it belongs to, and the year of its earliest known appearance in writing. Unlike the Unabridged version, the Collegiate Dictionary doesn't include synonyms or etymologies.

One very cool feature of the Merriam-Webster dictionary is that you can tap any word on a definition page to look up *its* definition. For example, in the figure on the right, if you were to tap the word *incapable,* the app would display the definition page for *incapable.*

Best features

An age-old quandary asks how you can look up the spelling of a word if you don't know how to spell it. In addition to being able to speak the word you want to look up, the Merriam-Webster dictionary offers two more ways that you can find the spelling of a word.

The first is a Similar Words feature: Type in how you *think* a word might be spelled, and you'll see a list of similarly spelled words. I typed in the intentionally misspelled *gage,* and received a long list of possible matches. The word I was looking for, *gauge,* appeared about halfway down the list.

The other way to find the proper spelling of a word is to use the Wildcard search feature. Use the "*" symbol (asterisk) to stand in for any number of letters, and the "?" symbol to replace a single letter. For instance, I searched for *franch** to find the correct spelling of the word *franchise.*

Worst features

With so many decent free dictionary apps — not to mention all those free dictionary Web sites — it's difficult to justify paying $25 for a dictionary app, unless you really need the features it offers.

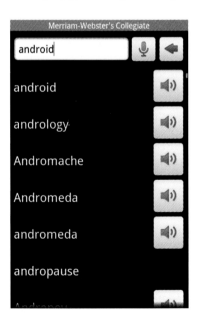

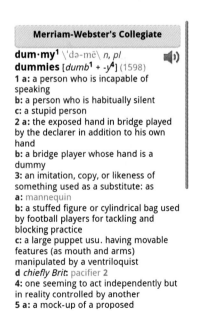

Recalls.gov
Free

Lately, it seems like product recalls are happening fast and furious. In fact, in the week preceding my writing this, 20 recalls were issued, according to the U.S. government's Recalls.gov Web site (www. recalls.gov). Most of these were food recalls, but there were also a few baby products, vehicles, and other items.

Whether it's shoddy manufacturing, imported products with unknown substances, or counterfeit items, these products put people's safety at risk. If you have children in your home — as I do — you need to be especially vigilant. To help you do just that, the U.S. government has put your tax dollars to work and created an Android app that keeps you up to date on all the latest product recalls.

The default screen of the Recalls.gov app displays a list of the most recent product recalls from all categories. Tap the Show More Results button to see older recalls, or filter the list to display only those recalls from a particular category. Six federal agencies provide the information for Recalls.gov. Among them, the categories covered include child safety seats, consumer products, drugs, food, motor vehicles, and tires.

Tap a product recall from the list and a page opens with extensive details about the recall. The recall notices often include an explanation about why the product is being recalled, pictures of the affected product, what to do with the product, where you can get additional information, and contact information for the product's manufacturer or distributor.

 If you look at a product recall notice for an item that is typically purchased off the shelf, such as food or toys, scroll down to the bottom of the recall notice. These notices often include links to a Web page that has photos of the product labels.

If you want to see if a particular product has been recalled, type the product's information into the search text box. You can search all recalls or just those in a particular category. Even better, if the product you are searching for has a bar code on it, you can use Recall. gov's built-in bar code scanner to scan it.

Recalls.gov also includes a Tips section that provides common-sense advice on topics such as window guards, cribs, and ATVs. There's not much content in this section right now, but hopefully, subsequent updates will include more useful information.

Best features

If you purchase items at yard sales, swap meets, or consignment stores, being able to search the government's recalls database is a great to way to determine if a secondhand item is safe.

Worst features

Recalls.gov includes what would seem to be a very valuable feature: a Report Incident button. This is so you can report potentially unsafe products to the proper authorities. Unfortunately, this feature links out to external Web pages that are not optimized for the small display of an Android device. If you want to report an unsafe product, you're better off doing it from a Web browser on your computer.

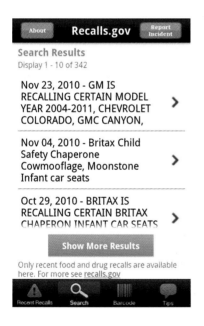 

WolframAlpha
$1.99

WolframAlpha is officially called a "computational knowledge engine." This means that it's not a *search engine*, it's an *answer engine*. Type in what you are looking for, and instead of getting a bunch of results with links that may or may not give you *some* of the information you're seeking, WolframAlpha gives you *the answer to your question*. I like to think of WolframAlpha as Google and Wikipedia squished together with a liberal sprinkling of the Encyclopedia Britannica and a bunch of university professors from every possible discipline.

When you type your query into WolframAlpha, it doesn't go out and search the Internet for the most relevant results, as most search engines do. Instead, WolframAlpha queries its own huge database of information, which is actually administered by live human beings! (What a concept for the 21 Century!) According to WolframAlpha (the company), WolframAlpha (the app) "contains 10+ trillion pieces of data, 50,000+ types of algorithms and models, and linguistic capabilities for 1000+ domains." And this vast store of knowledge is continually growing.

You can ask WolframAlpha virtually any question or seek almost any kind of information, and there's a very good chance it will give you an informed answer. WolframAlpha has tons of information about statistics and data analysis, the sciences, transportation, units and measurements, food and nutrition, and so on. WolframAlpha is from the folks who make the high-end computational software, Mathematica, so it shouldn't come as a surprise that WolframAlpha is also very good at solving equations.

The queries you throw at WolframAlpha needn't be in question form. For instance, type in "Hoboken" and hit the Go button. The results screen assumes you meant Hoboken, New Jersey, and lists all sort of stats, such as the city's population, the current time and weather there, some geographic properties, nearby cities, and even notable people born there (Frank Sinatra is probably Hoboken's most famous son). A number of these sections include buttons you can tap that expand to show even more data. If you still want more information, at the bottom of the screen are links for Source Information, Related Links, and Search the web.

Type in two company names and the results page gives you a side-by-side comparison of the two businesses, including a chart of their relative stock price history. Type in "star charts," and WolframAlpha displays a sky chart for your current location.

Another thing you can do is enter individual musical notes and WolframAlpha tells you what the corresponding chord is. Type in "peanut butter and jelly" and WolframAlpha displays all sorts of relevant nutritional facts.

On the answer screen, tap the Menu button and you'll see options to add the displayed results to your Favorites list or share them with your friends via means such as e-mail, text message, or Facebook. Also, all searches are saved to the History section, so you can easily revisit previous queries.

Best features

The extent of WolframAlpha's knowledge is mindboggling. The examples I cite here don't even begin to scratch the surface of the kinds of information WolframAlpha is capable of delivering. I wouldn't want to go up against WolframAlpha on *Jeopardy*!

Worst features

Of course WolframAlpha can't know *everything*. For instance, it didn't know where my missing socks were—although it responded, "Not sure, but wherever you find them, that's where they are."

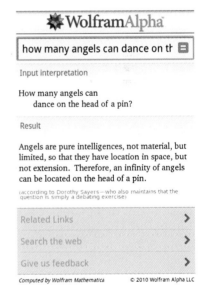

ConvertPad
Free (ad supported)

ConvertPad is a unit converter and algebraic calculator that includes a mind-boggling variety of different types of conversions it can compute. Common types of conversions are length, weight, and area. ConvertPad also incorporates a wealth of science-related unit conversions, such as entropy, thermal conductivity, and magnetic flux. There are a few surprises as well, such as cooking, typography, and lumber conversions. ConvertPad even includes currency (exchange rates) conversions. Perhaps the only conversion ConvertPad can't help you with is if you want to convert religions.

Free Dictionary Org
Free (ad supported)

Free Dictionary Org might not be the prettiest app to look at, but it harnesses the power of the Internet to collect detailed definitions. When you look up a word, the definitions come from a variety of online sources, such as the *Collaborative International Dictionary of English* and the WordNet lexical database. From these and other sources, you see definitions, pronunciations, and synonyms. Input your search via text or voice search; many definitions include spoken pronunciations (although they're not always accurate). You can even use Free Dictionary Org to search Google Images. If you want to export the text of a definition, install the free Catch Notes app from the Android Market and Free Dictionary Org seamlessly integrates with it.

Google Translate
Free

I have yet to find something that Google Translate can't translate. The quality of the translations probably won't pass muster at the United Nations, but they're good enough to get by on foreign soil or when trying to figure out a menu. Google Translate understands over 50 different languages, and can convert text between any of them. If you want to translate from Swahili to Yiddish, it can do it. You can input what you want to translate by typing it, pasting it from the clipboard, or even pulling it from your SMS messages. You can also speak what you want translated — or have someone else speak into the mic. But Google Translate's *pièce de résistance* is that it can actually speak the translated text. It might make for a very stilted conversation, but you could actually use Google Translate to have a conversation with someone who speaks a different language.

RealCalc Scientific Calculator
Free

I don't know what's more impressive — that RealCalc Scientific Calculator is a full-fledged scientific calculator, or that it's free. There isn't enough space here to list all the functions that RealCalc includes, but it can be used for simple arithmetic to trigonometric, logarithmic, and hyperbolic functions. It includes four display modes: normal, fixed decimal point, scientific notation, and engineering notation. Even if you don't need all these functions (or understand them), RealCalc includes a useful module that performs unit conversions for things like volume, energy, and data sizes. No student should be without this powerful calculator.

Wapedia
Free (ad supported)

Accessing Wikipedia from your Android device is as easy as pointing your browser to `m.wikipedia.org`. So then, you might be wondering why there are so many Wikipedia apps for Android. The answer is that they make searching and navigating Wikipedia much easier than using the Wikipedia site directly. The best Wikipedia app I've come across is Wapedia. When you search Wikipedia with Wapedia, you see a list of related matches, not just the main article. When you read an article, Wapedia breaks it up across multiple pages so that it's easier to manage, and a pop-up Contents window lets you jump directly to any section of the article. You also aren't limited to searching only Wikipedia articles; Wapedia gives you access to dozens of other online Wikis — ranging from the practical (Wiktionary) to the esoteric (Doctor Who Wiki).

14 Shopping and Dining Out

Amazon.com
Free

I'm old enough to remember that if you wanted to buy something, you essentially had two choices: You either went to an actual store to pick out and pay for your item, or you ordered it from a mail-order catalog. I have fond childhood memories of spending hours pouring over the Sears catalog, folding corners on page after page for all the toys that I wished I could get.

These days, there's little you can't purchase via online shopping, and Amazon.com, with its vast selection of product categories and its many merchant partners, has largely become the Sears catalog of the early 21st century. Amazon.com's Wish List has replaced the antiquated need to dog-ear pages to remember particular products. So is it any wonder that Amazon.com has a dedicated Android app that lets you peruse all Amazon.com has to offer and order products directly from your device?

Amazon.com's home screen is a simple affair, with a search box and recommendations based on your recent searches, such as the figure on the left. When you conduct a search, you get a list of matches, which you then can narrow down by limiting the search to a specific category. In the figure on the right, I restricted my search to the Music department.

When you tap an item, a page opens that includes relatively minimal information, such as a product image, a very brief description, its price, mention of how many merchant partners it's available from and what their lowest price is, average customer review ratings, and whether it's in stock. Tap any of these entries to see more detailed information. For instance, tap the average customer ratings to see all the customer reviews. At the bottom of the product page are buttons for Buy Now, Add to Cart, and Add to Wish List.

Press your device's Menu button to get access to your Shopping Cart, Wish List, Recommendations, and the Amazon Gold Box Deal of the Day. You can also access many of your account settings, such as Track Packages and View/Cancel Items or Orders.

Best features

With the Amazon Remembers feature, you can scan in a product's bar code to see if it is available on Amazon.com. Even better, you can take a photo of an actual object, and the app will try to recognize the item and determine if it's available from Amazon.com. Sometimes, you see search results right away; other times, it takes a few minutes. I am very impressed with the overall accuracy, as it correctly identifies far more items than it misses.

Worst features

Amazon.com's 1-Click Ordering is on by default — you don't need to sign in, and your order is processed as soon as you tap the Buy Now button. In my opinion, it's a bit *too* easy to purchase products this way.

I prefer to disable 1-Click Ordering in the app's settings, so that I must sign in and confirm my orders. This saves me the hassle of having to cancel an order if I accidentally tap the Buy Now button. It also affords me a few moments of reflection to ask myself if I really want to make this purchase.

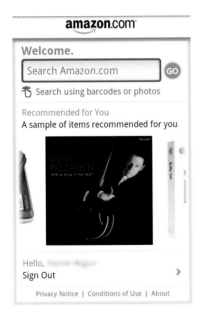

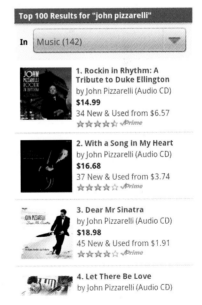

Grocery IQ
Free

On more than one occasion, I've been sent to the grocery store to pick up a quart of milk, only to return with a bag full of sundry items . . . but no milk. Those days are behind me now, because with the Grocery IQ app, I now arrive at the market knowing exactly what I need to pick up. A simple handwritten list would serve just as well, but the Grocery IQ app does many other things that are beyond the capabilities of mere pen and paper.

To best use Grocery IQ, you initially should spend some time populating the Favorites section with the groceries you buy on a regular basis. Tap the "+" at the top of the Favorites page (see the figure on the left), and a search box appears. Start typing the name of an item and Grocery IQ displays a list of suggested matches. You can pick an item from the list or create a new entry.

You can add items to the Favorites list in other ways, too: Tap the microphone icon to speak the item's name or scan in the item's bar code using your device's camera.

After you add your staples to the Favorites list, tap the arrow to the right of an item to input additional information about it, such as how many of the item to buy and how much you usually pay for it. Instead of quantity, you can input an item's weight, as I did with my entry for Apples in the figure on the right.

If you shop at more than one store, you can create entries for multiple stores and even assign specific items to a particular store.

When you're ready to go shopping, open the Favorites page and tap the check mark to the left of every item you want to add to your shopping list. After selecting everything, tap the Add to List button that appears at the top of the screen. All the items you selected are now added to the List page. You can modify items on the List page, such as changing quantities and adding additional items that weren't on the Favorites page.

While shopping, check each item off in the List as you place the item in your shopping cart. Grocery IQ keeps a tally of how many items are in your cart and what your expected checkout cost will be. Tap the Checkout button and all the items you checked disappear from the List and move to the History page.

Grocery IQ is from Coupons.com, so as you might expect, there is a Coupons page that lists lots of valuable coupons. If you find a coupon you want to use, tap it and the item automatically is added to your Coupons Cart. After you "clip" all the coupons you want, tap the View Cart button and then the Email Coupons button. You'll shortly receive an e-mail with instructions for how to print the coupons. If you have a Safeway or ShopRite club card, you can add coupons directly to your card.

Best features

Families with multiple shoppers can use the List Sharing feature, which allows you to sync the contents of Grocery IQ — including Favorites, List, Stores, and History — with other Grocery IQ users. Anytime a user makes changes, such as checking out an item from the List (because it was just purchased), this updates the Grocery IQ information for all the other users who share the list.

Worst features

The only club (or savings) cards that Grocery IQ currently supports are from ShopRite and from the Safeway family of stores, such as Vons and Carrs. It would be great if Grocery IQ supported club cards from more stores.

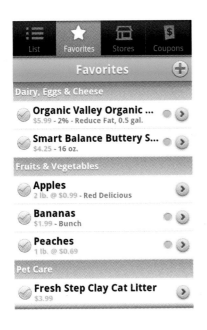

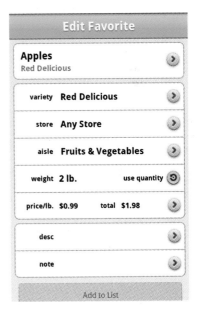

Shopper
Free

Let's say you're perusing the aisles of your favorite electronics store and you stumble across a product you've had your eye on for a while. You want know if you can find it cheaper elsewhere, and perhaps what other shoppers who've purchased it think of it. Maybe it's really a piece of junk!

You can find out all that and more just by using your handy-dandy Android device and the Shopper app. Launch Shopper and tap the Image search button. This fires up your device's camera, which you point at the bar code on the product's box. Shopper locks in on the bar code and performs a quick online search for the product. In mere seconds, Shopper spits out a list of places where you can purchase the product.

 If you get a lot of results, the search results can seem a little overwhelming. More often than not, however, you can tap the first entry to see the most relevant results. You can also filter your results with specific criteria, such as Free shipping and New items.

Tap the entry you want to see and Shopper takes you to the Overview screen for the product, which includes a picture of the item, the price range it sells for from the different sellers, how many sellers offer it, and how many user reviews are available of the product. You can also tap the star to save it as a favorite, or tap the Share button to send the listing via e-mail, Twitter, or Facebook.

Tap the Online button to see a list of all the sellers that offer the product online. You can sort the list by relevance, price, or seller rating. Tap the seller's listing and Shopper opens a page for the product on the seller's Web site, where you can purchase the item.

You can instead tap the Local button to see a list of all the stores nearby that sell the product; you can sort by distance or price.

If you want to know what other consumers say about the product, tap the Reviews button. Tap the Details button to get an in-depth description of the product, including specifications.

Best features

If you're looking for information about a book, audio CD, DVD, or video game, you don't even need the bar code. After you tap the Image search button, simply point your device's camera at the cover of the item; Shopper quickly scans the text or cover art and delivers the relevant results. You'll be amazed at how accurate the results are. (This is similar to Google Goggles, which you can read about in the Reference chapter. The similarity is not a coincidence —both apps are from the geniuses at Google Labs.)

Shopper's search capabilities don't end here. On Shopper's main screen, you can tap the Voice search button to speak what you are searching for. There's also a text search box if you want to type in your search. These are very helpful options when you don't have the product in front of you to scan.

Worst features

One thing Shopper can't do is scan QR codes. These are the codes that appear in this book and elsewhere that link to apps in the Android Market.

Shopper is also missing some useful features that you find in a handful of other bar-code scanner apps, such as the capability to create wish lists and set up price alerts. If these are important features to you, check out ShopSavvy or CNET Scan & Shop (both can also scan QR codes). Keep in mind that neither of these apps has Shopper's capability to scan cover art or do voice searches.

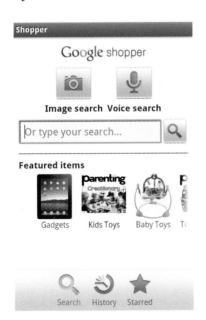

 **Where**
Free

My primary go-to app when I travel is aptly named Where. It helps me find a good lunch spot, the cheapest gas, and even what's happening in town if I want to blow off steam during my down time. You don't have to be a frequent traveler to benefit from what Where offers, though — you'll find plenty of information about all the places to go and things to do just outside your own front door.

Where's main screen includes buttons that give you instant access to information related to your current location, such as where to eat, drink, play, or catch the latest movies. Tap the local info button to see info such as news, traffic, and weather.

As the name indicates, the eat section provides a list of nearby restaurants. Search for all local restaurants or for specific cuisines, such as Asian, Indian, or Seafood. The drink section does the same but instead for bars, coffee shops, and the like, while the play section includes everything from miniature golf to music events. The search results lists show the places' names, addresses, and how far away they are from your location.

 You can also choose to see the search result locations on a map. If you tap a place's icon on the map, the available options are to call the restaurant or get driving directions.

When in list view, tap a place's entry to view more information about it (see the figure on the right), including what credit cards it takes (if any) and links to its menu and Web site (if available). You can also see its location on a map, get directions, read user reviews, write your own review, or save the entry as a Favorite or as a place you Want to Go. You can also share the listing with others via e-mail or an SMS text message.

If you have a pretty good idea of what you are looking for — or know the name of the place you are looking for, you can type it in using the search box at the top of Where's main screen.

 When you launch Where, it can get your current location from your device's GPS settings, you can enter a location manually, or you can use a previous location. Searching other areas is a great tool to use when planning a trip.

Looking for bargains? Where includes a Coupons section that provides electronic coupons for local, participating businesses. You can save the coupons to use later and even set Where to notify you when a coupon is about to expire.

The guides section is a great way to explore new places or even rediscover your own town. It includes "insider tips from local experts," on things like where to find the best spa treatments or outdoor places where you can enjoy the spring weather. Once you start saving Favorite places, the best bets section makes recommendations on places you should try that are similar to what you like.

Best features

You're not limited to just searching for places to eat, drink, or have fun. You can also search for places, such as grocery stores and hotels.

Worst features

I didn't find a lot of user reviews for the restaurants and shops near me — and I live in a large urban community. If you want to see what others have to say about an establishment, use Yelp (also reviewed in this chapter), which contains tons of user-supplied reviews.

Yelp
Free

If you put a lot of stock in the advice of your friends when it comes to picking a place to eat or shop, then you're going to love Yelp. Between the Yelp Android, iPhone, and Palm apps, as well as the Yelp Web site (www.yelp.com), "Yelpers" have posted more than 12 million reviews about local businesses. You can also easily join the fray and add your opinions about your local establishments.

If you're looking for user reviews of a specific business, type its name into the search text box on Yelp's home screen. If you're just looking for a good dry cleaner or a decent place to eat that's close by, tap the home screen's Nearby button (see the figure on the left) to see a list of categories to pick from, such as Restaurants, Drugstores, or Pets. Many of these categories have subcategories you can pick from to help you further narrow down your search; for instance, under Nightlife, you can search for just the local Karaoke joints.

A search results list appears, displaying the closest locations at the top of the page. Each item in the list includes the name of the business, a picture, the address, how far away it is from your present location, and how expensive it tends to be. Probably the most important bit of information for each listing is its average user rating, which is displayed as a rating of up to five stars.

When you tap on a listing, you see more detailed information, including the business hours and the closest transportation options. You can see the business on a map, get directions, or tap on the phone number to call them if your device is a phone. Lots of helpful tidbits appear at the bottom of several listings, such as if the establishment accepts credit cards, is kid friendly, and if it's good for groups. Tap the Read Reviews button to see all the reviews that other Yelpers have posted about the establishment.

A ribbon runs across the middle of the page, which includes buttons for Add Tip, Add Photo, Check In, Draft Review, and Bookmark (see the figure on the right). You can post your own brief tip, such as "get there before 9 a.m. on weekends to avoid the rush," or upload your own photo of the place. Tap the Check In button to let your fellow Yelpers know you're there right now (you can choose to post this on Facebook and Twitter as well). If you want to write your own review of the place, tap the Draft Review button, assign it a rating, and start your critiquing. You can also save the listing to your Bookmarks.

Best features

You can find out what's around you by using Yelp's cool Monocle feature. Tap the Monocle button from Yelp's home screen; in a few moments, the screen displays a live image of what your device's camera sees. Using the device's GPS and compass, Monocle is location aware. Point the camera at a business and Monocle overlays a small box that includes the location's name, type of business, average rating, and its distance from you. Tap the box to see the detailed listing for that business. Monocle also displays information about other nearby businesses that you might not be able to see from where you are standing.

This is a technology called "augmented reality," and it's used by a number of apps, including Google Goggles, which I discuss in the Reference chapter. If you want to explore augmented reality in more detail, check out the Layar app (free in the Android Market), which overlays scads of information about all sorts of things — not just local businesses — over the images of many real-world places and things.

Worst features

As with all user-supplied reviews, take what you read with a grain of salt. Sometimes people have hidden agendas or axes to grind. Don't use one bad review as a reason to avoid giving an establishment your business.

The Coupons App
Free (subscription required)

Coupon clippers, toss your scissors and rejoice. With The Coupons App, let the coupons come to you. Even better, you don't have to print them out; just call them up on the screen when you're at the cashier.

You can save coupons, share them via e-mail or social networking, and even save them to your calendar with reminders on the days they expire. The Coupons App helps you find a coupon's nearest store, and even gives you the phone number and driving directions.

The Coupons App is free, but in order to unlock all of its features, you must buy a subscription, which starts at $0.99 per month.

Craigslist Notification
Free (ad supported)

Who needs classified ads in the back of newspapers, when you've got Craigslist (`craigslist.org`)? Chances are if you're looking to buy a used item, someone else is looking to sell it on Craigslist.

Create a search query by supplying keywords and choosing a category (such as "for sale"). You can fine-tune your query by selecting a subcategory (such as "antiques"), supplying minimum and maximum price filters, designating specific regions to search, and searching only listings that include images. You can even create multiple searches if you are looking to buy several items. Craigslist Notification conducts its searches in the background, downloads the ads that match your search queries, and notifies you when new ads are available.

Official eBay Android App
Free

You're selling 16 items and bidding on 6 on eBay, but you're going to be away from your computer for a few hours. What will you do? The official eBay Android app to the rescue! Sellers can track items they are selling, see what has and hasn't sold, and what's scheduled to go on sale. Buyers can watch items, track their bids, and see what they have and haven't won. You can set the eBay app to send you notifications when you've been outbid and when a watched item's auction is about to end. With the eBay app, you'll never miss another auction.

WootWatcher
Free

Everybody loves a good bargain, and if you like to do your shopping online, you've probably heard of Woot (`www.woot.com`); perhaps you've even purchased items from Woot. Woot offers a different discounted or refurbished item every day; most often, it's some sort of consumer electronics. Woot also has sister sites that sell shirts (`shirt.woot.com`), discontinued products (`sellout.woot.com`), wine (`wine.woot.com`), and kids' items (`kids.woot.com`). WootWatcher keeps an eye on the different Woot sites and notifies you when new items are for sale. Each Woot site gets its own page in WootWatcher, which includes a picture of the product. Tap the image to read the amusing and often irreverent product descriptions. At the bottom of the listing are the official (and not so humorous) specs.

Zagat to Go '10
$9.99 US

Zagat offers some of the most reliable restaurant reviews and ratings. Similar to Yelp (also in this chapter), Zagat relies on the opinions of diners to form its ratings. Although Yelp can serve up an overwhelming collection of user-supplied reviews for a single establishment, the Zagat editors painstakingly synthesize all the input they receive into one concise review of a restaurant. I looked at the 2010 edition, which included more than 40,000 reviews of restaurants, nightspots, hotels, and stores, from nearly every major U.S. city. You can see what's nearby, or search by neighborhood or cuisine. You can sort search results by any of the rating criteria, restaurant name, or distance from your present location.

15 Social Networking

eBuddy Messenger
Free

If you collect numerous instant messaging (IM) accounts from a variety of IM services, like I do, you need an IM client that lets you connect to the different IM services with all of your accounts at the same time. Of the numerous Android apps that do this, eBuddy Messenger is my favorite.

Use eBuddy Messenger to connect to accounts on AIM, ICQ, Facebook, Google Talk, Hyves, MSN, MySpace, and Yahoo!. If you have multiple accounts through the same service, such as an AIM account for work and a separate AIM account for your friends, you can sign in with all your accounts simultaneously.

All of your buddies from the different accounts appear in a single list on the Buddies screen (see the figure on the left). By default, the list sorts by buddy name, but you can have your buddies appear by group or account. You can also set whether your offline buddies appear in the buddies list as well.

To start chatting with a buddy, tap on the buddy's entry on the Buddies screen, and a Chat screen automatically opens. Type your message in the box at the bottom of the screen and tap the Send button (see the figure on the right).

You can have multiple chats with different buddies going on at the same time. Tap the Chats tab to see the Chats screen, which lists all of your open chats. If you are in an active chat, swipe the screen left or right to scroll through to your other open chats.

When someone sends you a chat message, eBuddy Messenger notifies you in several different ways: It plays a sound, vibrates the device, and flashes the device's LED light (you can disable any of these settings). It also places an alert in your device's status bar.

In order to use eBuddy Messenger, you first have to create a free eBuddy ID account. If you have multiple IM accounts, it might be quicker to first set up your eBuddy ID and associated IM accounts on the eBuddy Web site (www.ebuddy.com), instead of doing it all from the eBuddy Messenger app on your device. After everything is set up on the eBuddy Web site, all you have to do is log into the eBuddy Messenger app on your device with your eBuddy ID, and it automatically adds all of your IM accounts.

Best features

eBuddy Messenger supports multitasking, so it will work in the background while you run other apps. In fact, you can set eBuddy Messenger to automatically launch and log in to your IM accounts whenever your device starts up.

Worst features

You can't copy or save the text of your chats.

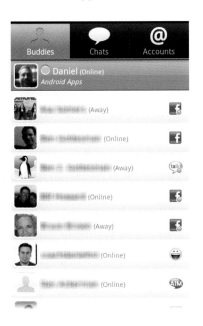

Facebook for Android
Free

Facebook has more than 500 million active users, which means that approximately 7.26 percent of the world population uses Facebook. To say that Facebook is popular is a gross understatement. I'm even willing to bet that *you* are a Facebook user. Assuming that I'm correct and that you'd like to access Facebook from your Android device, Facebook has the solution with its very own Facebook for Android app.

Facebook for Android's main screen is smartly laid out with many of the key features you're most likely to use within easy reach (see the figure on the left). The main screen includes buttons for your News Feed, Profile, Friends, Messages, Places, Groups, Events, Photos, and Requests. The bottom of the screen has a strip of thumbnails of recent photos and videos posted by your friends. You can scroll through the thumbnails or tap one to see its associated post.

Buttons at the top of the screen are for sharing your status and for searching for people. When you tap the button for sharing your status, it does the exact same thing as when you tap the News Feed button: It opens the News Feed page with a "What's on your mind?" text box on top (see the figure on the right).

To the right of the "What's on your mind?" text box is the Share button, and to the left of the text box is the Upload Photo button. When you tap the Upload Photo button, a window pops up that lets you choose an existing photo or capture a photo using your device's camera. After you choose or snap a photo, you can add a caption and choose an existing album to post the photo to.

If you don't select an album, Facebook for Android automatically adds the photo to your Mobile Uploads album.

When you scroll down the News Feed page to see more posts, the "What's on your mind?" text box scrolls off the page. So if you want to send out a status update, scroll back up to the top of the page — or switch to your Profile page, where there's also a "What's on your mind?" text box on top. The Profile screen has tabs for your Wall, Info, and Photos. The Messages screen has tabs for Messages, Updates, and Sent.

The Places screen displays a feed of all the places that your friends have recently checked into. Tap the Check In button in the upper-right corner of the screen to broadcast your location to your friends. When you tap Check In, a list of nearby locations appears. If the location you want doesn't appear, you can search for it. If the location still doesn't appear, you can add it manually.

Use the settings to control how often the News Feed refreshes (you can do a manual refresh at any time) and configure the notification options. You can choose to be notified when you receive messages, friend requests, and event invites. In addition to notifications in your device's status bar, you can opt to be notified by having your device vibrate, flash the LED, and play a ringtone.

Best features

The smart design of Facebook for Android makes it easy to quickly find whatever you are looking for.

Worst features

A number of features are missing from Facebook for Android; in my opinion, the most egregiously absent feature is the capability to chat with other Facebook users. That said, Facebook (the company) frequently updates the app; it's possible that chat will be an integral part of the app in the future.

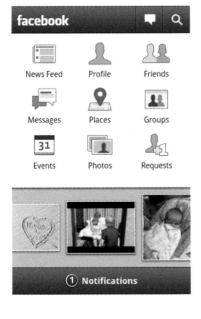
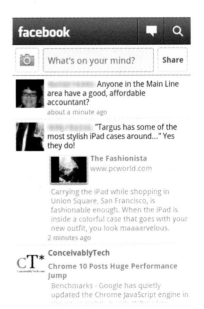

Family GPS Tracker
Free

You can't put a price on peace of mind when it comes to knowing that your family is safe and sound; but, with their Family GPS Tracker Android app, the folks at Life360 seem to think that this sense of comfort should be free. Family GPS Tracker lets you see the real-time locations of your individual family members on a map and send and receive nearly instant check-in and help-needed request messages.

In order to track your family, everyone needs to install the Family GPS Tracker on his or her mobile phone (you can get a free iPhone version of the app as well). If you want to track family members who don't carry mobile phones — such as toddlers — you can purchase a Zoombak GPS tracking device from www.life360.com for each of them. Each device costs $99.

When you set up an account using the app (or on the Life360 Web site), you are assigned a FamilyID number. As you add family members to your account, everybody uses the same FamilyID number, but is assigned a unique PIN (personal identification number). When you set up Family GPS Tracker on your family members' phones, just input the FamilyID number and appropriate PIN to link a phone to particular user.

Once everyone's phone is set up, launch the app and in a few short seconds, you see a map with your location pinpointed on it. The bottom of the screen shows icons for each of your family members (see the figure on the left). Tap a family member's icon and that person's location appears on the map. Tap the location marker on the map for that person, and another screen displays the family member's current status (Safe, Help, or Unknown), the last time the status was updated, the address of the person's location, and how recently the location was updated. The latitude and longitude of the family member's coordinates and how accurate the GPS signal is also appear.

 You also see icons on the map for hospitals, police stations, fire departments, and registered sex offenders.

The bottom of the map screen includes Check In and Panic buttons. Tap the Check In button to update your status as Safe. You also have the option to send out an e-mail notification of your safe status, which includes your current location. Tap the Panic button to change your status to Help, and to send out e-mail, text, and automated voice call blasts to your emergency contacts (see the figure on the right). Immediately after the alert is sent out, you're given the option to call 911. Phone call and e-mail Panic alerts include the sender's address, time sent, accuracy of GPS signal, and coordinates. Panic alert text messages include only the sender's address.

TIP

In order for Family GPS Tracker to work, you must enable location services in your phone's settings. Also, if you use a task manager app, such as SystemPanel (reviewed in Chapter 17), make sure to create an exception for Family GPS Tracker in the task manager app, so that when you terminate running tasks, you don't accidentally disable the Family GPS Tracker app.

Best features

Family GPS Tracker is a great way for kids to check in and let their parents know that they're actually where they are supposed to be.

Worst features

To add additional emergency contact information to your account, such as phone numbers for automated voice calls and text messages, you can only enter this information on the Life360 Web site.

Foursquare
Free

Foursquare is a social networking service where users advertise their location to their friends. For some, it's a great way to find out about cool, new places to explore as they learn about locations from their friends. For others, it's a way to brag about how cool *they* are, because of all the *awesome* places they hang out. For others, Foursquare is a kind of real-world game, where they earn "badges" for visiting certain locations (see the figure on the left).

In fact, the ultimate goal for many Foursquare users is to become the "Mayor" of a location — a badge awarded to the user who has visited a location the most in a 60-day period. Many other kinds of badges are also awarded to users, including the "Newbie" badge, which you get after you "Check In" to your first location.

To best use Foursquare, you need to be mobile, so the ideal platform for accessing Foursquare is from a mobile device, such as a phone. The Foursquare Android app is perfect for this.

The app is broken up into five main sections:.

- ✔ **Friends:** This is where you see what your friends have been up to recently. You see where they've been, when they were there, and any comments they "shouted" when they checked in (see the figure on the right).

- ✔ **Places:** This screen displays all the locations that are close to your present location. Tap a location's entry to open a new screen that lets you check in to that location, leave a tip, add a to-do, see who the location's current mayor is, view any tips that users have posted about the location, and see the location on a map.

- ✔ **Tips:** Here you see tips that your friends and other Foursquare users have posted about nearby locations. You often see tips about what's the best item on a restaurant's menu or reasons why you should avoid a business.

- ✔ **To-Do:** To-Do's are essentially reminders to yourself that you want to check out a location. Any recent To-Do's you've added appear here. View your Recent To-Do's and any To-Do's for Nearby locations. You can also remove items from your To-Do list and mark that you've done a To-Do.

✔ **Me:** The Me page is where you can see your stats, such as the badges you've earned, how many Check Ins you've accumulated, and if you have any pending friend requests.

Before you go willy-nilly and check in to every possible location you visit and try to rack up as many badges as possible, keep in mind that all information you disseminate is public. Think twice before you advertise to the world that you just checked-in to Harriet's Electrolysis Clinic. When you announce to the world that you're out and about, you're also saying that you aren't currently at home. Some unsavory characters might see your post and decide that it's an opportune time to visit your presumably unoccupied home and liberate it of your prized possessions.

Best features

Some businesses offer discounts to users who check in to their locations through Foursquare. Companies that have done this include American Eagle Outfitters, Gap, and Steve Madden.

Worst features

Many users like to link Foursquare to their Facebook and Twitter accounts, so that their Foursquare check-ins also automatically post on Facebook and Twitter. Unfortunately, you can't set this up in the Foursquare app. Instead, you have to configure these settings on the Foursquare Web site (foursquare.com).

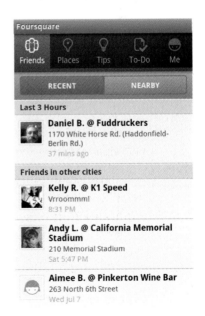

Twidroyd Pro for Twitter
$3.99 US

When it comes to Twitter apps for Android — and there are a lot of them — none of them holds a candle to Twidroyd Pro for Twitter. Hands-down, Twidroyd has the slickest interface, the most robust features, and the greatest number of user-configurable settings I've seen. In fact, Twidroyd is even more powerful than some Twitter clients for desktop computers.

Upon first glance, you don't necessarily realize the full capabilities of Twidroyd, because they are hidden just below the surface. The Timeline page looks very much like the timeline of many other Twitter clients, as seen in the figure on the left. Tap an entry in the timeline, however, and the Tweet Options window that appears in the figure in the right opens. From this window, you can do any number of things, such as launch your device's Web browser to see a linked page, reply to a tweet, see a user's profile, or send out a retweet.

Back on the main screen are tabs for a Mentions page, Direct Messages page, and a Search page. On the Search page, you can search for tweets, users, and nearby tweets. You can also search using the PostUp engine, which displays results culled specifically from highly ranked tweeters.

 While viewing the Timeline or Mentions page, tap your device's Menu button to make a "Jump To Top" button appear. Tap this button to send the display instantly back to the top of the list.

There's one more tab on the main screen; it opens the More page (this is the tab with the three dots in the figure on the left). The More page has 18 buttons; they perform functions such as displaying suggested users to follow, recent trends, and nearby tweets. Here you can also manage follower requests, mute users (which suppresses a user's tweets from appearing in your timeline), manage lists, and even manage multiple Twitter accounts.

Hidden all the way at the bottom of the More page is the Settings button. Here you find a plethora of settings for notifications, display options, photo and video posting, URL shortening, and geolocation, just to name a few. Examples of just how detailed the settings can be are that you can: set Twidroyd to start when the device boots up; control under which specific conditions notifications will be sent; change the app's skin; change the size of the font; configure Twidroyd to display real names instead of Twitter usernames; disable profile images; select photo, video, and URL shortening services; and automatically annotate your tweets with location information.

Best features

In the figure on the right, you might have noticed a "LivePreview" entry at the top of the Tweet Options screen. When you choose this option, it places the selected tweet at the top of the page and displays a tweet's linked Web page or media in a large window below the tweet. Back and forth arrows let you stay in LivePreview mode and scroll through the other tweets in your timeline. Even better, when you view the timeline with the device in landscape mode, the display automatically switches to LivePreview mode with the timeline on the left side of the screen and the preview window on the right.

Worst features

I've yet to find anything about Twidroyd that I don't like, although some users might actually find all the options overwhelming.

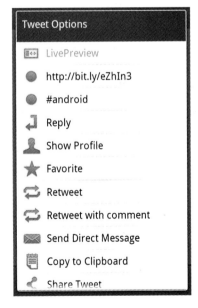

AppAware – Find Hot Apps
Free

If you want to know what apps other folks are running on their Android devices, fire up AppAware. The Live page shows a real-time feed of what apps other AppAware users are installing, updating, and uninstalling (although you have to manually refresh the screen to update). You can also see what apps the users nearby you are adding and deleting. My favorite page is the Top page, which displays the most popular installed, updated, and removed apps within the last hour, day, or week, for all AppWare users. Tap an app's entry to open a page that shows details about the app, its overall popularity, tags that other AppAware users assigned to it (keep an eye out for helpful tags such as "fake" or "scam"), and a link to the app in the Android Market.

Bump
Free

Bump is an ingenious way to quickly share contacts, photos, and apps with other Android users. Just launch Bump on both devices, select what you want to share, and gently bump your respective hands together, which are holding your devices. A window pops up and asks you to confirm the transfer. It's that easy!

You can also share contacts and photos with iPhone users who are running the iPhone version of Bump. Unfortunately, although iPhone users can also share music and calendar entries with each other, the Android version of Bump currently does not support this. The folks at Bump Technologies, however, are hard at work trying to add this functionality and other goodies to the Android version of Bump — so keep an eye out for updates with more features.

DroidIn Pro
$1.99 US

LinkedIn is a social network for professionals — it's a great way to network and look for work. Unless you are retired, too young to have a job, or a member of the idle rich, you should join LinkedIn (Basic membership is free). Surprisingly, there aren't many Android apps for LinkedIn, and LinkedIn itself has yet to release an official app.

Of the few LinkedIn apps available, DroidIn Pro is the superior choice. It gives you access to all of your contacts' information as well as your own profile. You can see your contacts' status updates as well as post your own status updates. You can even search LinkedIn for people and companies, which is what many people use LinkedIn the most often for.

When I looked at DroidIn 4 LinkedIn, it was still in beta, and there were a few things it couldn't do, such as access your LinkedIn Inbox and Groups. You also couldn't edit your profile. The developer has been making frequent updates and the app keeps getting better and better, so I wouldn't be surprised to see at least some of these features available with future updates.

GetGlue
Free

If Foursquare (reviewed earlier in the chapter) is the social network for social butterflies, then I like to think of GetGlue as the social network for folks who get most their entertainment without leaving their homes. The GetGlue app connects you to the GetGlue network, where you share your preferences for TV shows, movies, music, books, and video games with other like-minded users. You can check in, letting everybody know what you are watching, listening to, or reading. You can see a Stream of what other users are presently up to. You can also rate movies, books, and the like and see what ratings others have assigned to them. Like Foursquare, the more you participate, the more rewards you get. In the case of GetGlue, you are awarded stickers for your frequent participation.

StumbleUpon
Free

StumbleUpon gives new meaning to surfing the Web. Just tap the Start Stumbling! button and StumbleUpon launches a random Web page for you to view. It picks pages based on your favorite topics (which you have to configure on the StumbleUpon Web site at www.stumbleupon.com) and pages that you've previously rated. You can also stumble through Flickr photos, YouTube videos, news stories, and even Android apps. StumbleUpon is a great way to discover new things on the Web that will tickle your fancy.

16 Sports

 GPSCaddy
£12.99

Not every golfer can have a caddy whispering in his ears, warning about the water hazard or tricky dogleg lying in wait down the fairway. With your Android device and the GPSCaddy app installed, you'll know about every hole's feature that sits between the tee and the green.

GPSCaddy is a location-aware app that uses your device's GPS to determine its exact location. After you load the map for the course you are playing and tell GPSCaddy which hole you're on, it displays a Fairway View with your location as a blue dot on a satellite photo of the hole. It also displays a straight line from where you are standing to the center of the green (see the figure on the left).

The map also shows how far you are from the front, middle, and back of the green. If the hole has any hazards, such as a bunker, the map indicates your distance to them. As you take your strokes and work your way down the fairway, the distance markers for these features update to adjust for your new position. When you're close to the green, you can select Green View, which zooms in on the green and shows just the three distance markers for the green.

GPSCaddy can track the scores of up to four players. At the end of each hole, tap the Next Hole button and you're prompted to enter the scores for all the players. After you input the scores and tap Enter, GPSCaddy automatically displays the map for the next hole.

 GPSCaddy helps you figure out how far your shots go, too. Before you take your shot, tap the Shot Distance button. Take your shot, make your way to where your ball landed, and then tap the Shot Distance button again. GPSCaddy quickly calculates the distance between these two locations and displays it in a dialog box.

Instead of the default Graphics View, you can choose to see each hole's information using GPSCaddy's Text View feature. In Text View, you just see the features listed and your distance to them, displayed as white letters and numbers on a black background. If it's very sunny and difficult to see your device's screen, this mode might be easier to see than the Graphics View.

Before you plunk down £12.99 (roughly $20 US) for GPSCaddy, check the list of available course maps on the GPSCaddy Web site at `www.caltonhillgolf.com/showCourses.php` to make sure that maps exist for the courses you typically play. You can download up to five courses. If maps don't exist for your courses, you can request that they be created — although there's no guarantee that your request will be honored. Alternatively, you can create your own course maps using the GPSCaddy app's Create Course tool while you're out on the course.

Best features

Users who create their own courses can upload them to GPSCaddy's course map server. If the uploaded courses are approved, they become available for all other GPSCaddy users to download and use. Encouraging the GPSCaddy community to upload courses is perhaps the most effective way to build up the course map library.

Worst features

Unfortunately, many courses don't have maps available. Unless you create your own or have faith that GPSCaddy's developer will take pity on your request to create one for you, GPSCaddy won't do you any good out on the links. If that's the case, see if the $1.99 SkyDroid – Golf GPS (`www.skydroid.net/courses.php`) or $14.95 FreeCaddie Pro Golf GPS (`http://freecaddie.com/CourseCreatorSelectCourseForViewing.aspx`) apps have maps for the courses you play.

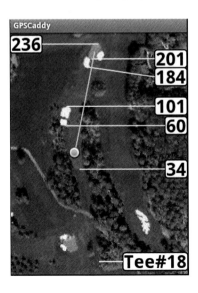

MLB.com At Bat

$14.99 US during season (Free during off-season)

MLB.com At Bat focuses on only one sport, baseball, but it does so very well. And it better, because this is the *official* Android app for all of major league baseball.

When you launch MLB.com At Bat, it displays the Scoreboard screen, which gives you a brief overview of every game that's going on that day (see the figure on the left). Each game listed shows the score, the inning, bases occupied, number of outs, who's pitching, who's at bat, and even the current count of balls and strikes. You can actually watch numerous games at the same time this way. If the game hasn't started yet, you see the start time, each team's season-to-date record of wins and losses, the starting pitchers, and the pitchers' stats.

Tap and hold an active game on the Scoreboard page to hear a live radio broadcast of the game. You can pick from several broadcasts. There will always be at least two available — one broadcast from the home team, and one from the visiting team. You can leave the app to do other things with your device, and the game's audio will continue to play in the background.

If you want to see pitch-by-pitch details of the game as it happens, tap the game's entry on the Scoreboard screen, which opens the Game page (see the figure on the right). Icons for balls and strikes appear next to the image of a batter — the batter appears on whichever side of the plate the actual batter is standing. Below that are stats, such as how many pitches the pitcher has thrown, the batter's RBI, and who's on deck.

The bottom of the screen shows the continuously updated plays for the current inning. Here you see information such as if a batter gets on base or strikes out, how fast the pitches are, and even if the manager visits the mound and changes pitchers. This same information also appears on the Plays screen, where you can see all the plays for each inning.

Tap the Box tab to see the current box score for the two teams and all of their players. In the box score, tap a player's name to see a Player Card that shows the player's complete stats. The Field screen shows all the current defensive and offensive players on the playing field.

The Video page continually updates throughout the game with clips and highlights.

Shortly after a game finishes, a condensed video of the game appears on the Video page — these videos can be as much as 20 minutes in length. You also can see the box scores, plays, and videos for any finished game — even those that were played months ago.

Additional features are available via the Menu button, such as the current standings for the AL, NL, AL wildcard, and NL wildcard teams. You can also see the latest baseball headlines, or choose to see news stories for a particular team.

Best features

Streaming audio and live play-by-play coverage for every regular and post-season game on your Android device is a nirvana for any baseball fan who can't be at the game or in front of a TV.

Worst features

The app's live radio broadcasts often lag a couple of minutes behind the play-by-play data, which can make it confusing to follow a game. I recommend either watching the real-time stats or listening to a game, but not both at the same time. Another downer is that no live video streams are available for the games.

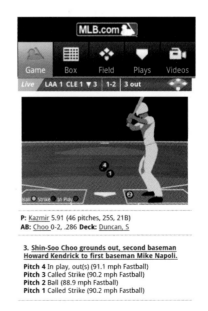

Satski
£5.99

The next time you hit the slopes, bring along your Android device with Satski installed on it, and you'll wonder how you ever skied or snowboarded without it. As its name implies, Satski is a GPS tracking app for skiers; but it does far more than just show where you are on a map of a mountain.

To get started with Satski, you first have to choose the resort you're skiing. It includes many popular resorts in Europe, North America, and the Asian Pacific region, and more resorts are being added over time. After you select the resort, it downloads to your device. As soon as it loads, Satski displays a map of the resort, such as Kicking Horse, British Columbia, in the figure on the left.

The scrollable and zoomable map displays the resort's trails, their difficulty levels, ski lifts, and gondolas. The map also lists many of the resort features, such as lodges, restaurants, and bars — some of which are highlighted with yellow squares. Tap the square to see more information, such as the name of the establishment, a photograph of it, and a phone number. You can also call up a complete list of the resort's information from the Menu button.

Your location appears as a red circle on the map. You could peruse the map to figure out how to get from point A to point B, but there is an easier way. Choose Satski's Navigate option, and select your starting and ending points from the available locations, which include the resort's features, lifts, and gondolas. If you'd rather not be challenged during this journey, you can choose to avoid red and black runs (see the figure on the right). Tap the Show Route button and the map displays the quickest route, via trails and lifts.

If you want to see where you've already been for the day, choose the Replay option to see all the trails you've skied and lifts you've used. Select the Stats option to see how much distance you've covered, your average and max speeds, and your altitude.

After you're back in front of your computer, you can copy the data off your device using the free Stats Viewer application (for Windows PCs, downloadable from www.satsportsgps.com) to see detailed stats, including information for each run. You can also replay the day's travails on a map of the resort or with Google Earth.

If you get in trouble on the slopes and need assistance, Satski can help. Select the Emergency option and Satski gives you the phone number for the resort's mountain rescue as well as your location's precise latitude and longitude.

Best features

Satski includes a Live Services feature that sends you updates on things such as the weather and snow forecasts, trail conditions, and lift closures. Perhaps the coolest feature is Buddy Tracking. If your friends are also using Satski, you can see each other's real-time locations on the map.

Worst features

If you ski at several resorts, you need to acclimate yourself to a variety of different, inconsistent map styles. Some maps are easy to read and intuitive, while others can be confusing to figure out.

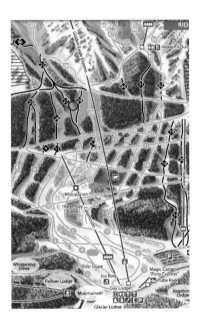

 **SportsTap**
Free (ad supported)

You don't have to be a sports nut to appreciate SportsTap. Its easy-to-navigate interface and tough-to-beat price (free!) make it the ideal app even if you just want to check on a score or see a team's schedule every once in a while. That said, crazed sports fans who can never get enough up-to-date information about their favorite teams will love SportsTap for its wealth of data and capability to deliver timely updates.

SportsTap covers many of the major sports that are followed in North America, including professional football (NFL and CFL), baseball, basketball, and hockey. Additional coverage includes NCAA football and basketball, auto racing (NASCAR, Formula 1, and Indy car racing), golf, and tennis. SportsTap even covers Futbol, which we Yanks call "soccer."

 SportsTap is somewhat limited in its international sports coverage. If SportsTap doesn't include your team or sport (such as rugby or cricket), check out Google Scoreboard, which has greater global coverage but isn't quite as snazzy as SportsTap in appearance or functionality.

If games are currently taking place for a covered sport, a red circle appears on the icon for that sport on SportsTap's home page. In the figure on the left, nine major league baseball games and five NHL hockey games were taking place when I captured the screenshot.

When you tap on any of the icons, a screen appears that shows summary boxes of all the games currently taking place for that sport, including the current score and inning (or quarter, period, or half, depending on the sport). The figure on the right shows summary boxes for nine active baseball games, plus the day's games that were already over. Games that haven't started yet display their expected start times and the TV channels the game will be on for the team's local markets (if available). Games that are finished show the final score.

Tap a summary box for a game in progress or a finished game to see a detailed scoring summary and list of all the plays or team comparisons. Tap a game that hasn't started yet to see the AccuScore data (a simulated game projection with odds), matchup data, and a detailed game preview.

Back on the game summaries page for each sport, you also see related photos from the news and top news stories. Tap any of these items to see more detail. At the bottom of the page, you can access information on the sport's standings, transactions, season leaders, team statistics, and team schedules. You can also navigate to previous days to see past scores, or ahead to future dates to see scheduled games.

The LocalTap icon on the home page shows you all the major sporting events that are taking place within a 50-, 100-, or 200-mile radius.

Best features

You can select teams to add to your Favorites from a combination of teams from the NFL, MLB, NBA, NHL, NCAA Football, and NCAA Men's Basketball. SportsTap then provides you with notifications when your Favorite teams' games start and end, and delivers regular score updates. You can set the update frequency to between 1 and 60 minutes.

Worst features

The information, such as the score for a game in progress, is sometimes slow to come in. There might be a delay of several minutes between real time and what SportsTap reports.

Yahoo! Fantasy Football
Free (ad supported)

Aside from *watching* sports, one of the great American pastimes has become *participating* in fantasy sports leagues, where fans manage virtual teams, pitting them against other players' fictional lineups.

One of the more popular destinations for fantasy sports is Yahoo!, which hosts fantasy leagues for a number of sports, including baseball, basketball, and hockey. But perhaps the most popular fantasy sport has to be football, and if you participate in a Yahoo! Fantasy Football league, you can manage your teams and players from your Android device with the Yahoo! Fantasy Football app.

The first thing you probably want to do is check the league's standings. The figure on the left shows the standings for the teams in my fantasy football league. Select a team to view that team's roster (see the figure on the right).

You can see your own team's players by selecting the My Team button on the bottom of the screen. Here you see all of your starters and benched players. Tap on a player's entry to see his stats from the last week, current season, and previous season, as well as notes about his recent performance. For any player who's not on the Can't-Cut List, a Drop button sits at the bottom of a player's stats screen. If you don't like a player's performance or he's injured, tap the Drop button to remove him from your roster. (The best 30 to 40 players in the league are automatically placed on the Can't-Cut List. You can't remove these players from your roster even when they're injured. This is a setting, however, that your league's Commissioner can disable.)

 The icon that looks like a yellow notepad with the red star next to a player's listing (in the figure on the right) indicates that there are notes about that player that have posted within the last 24 hours. The "Q" next to Reggie Wayne's name means that his current status is questionable. Other codes you might see are "D" (doubtful), "P" (probable), "IR" (injured reserve), or "DTD" (day-to-day).

Make changes to your roster by tapping the Edit Lineup button in the upper-right corner of the My Team page. Here you can move players from the starters to the bench and vice versa. You add players to your roster from the Players page, where you can search for players by their names or search for players by position.

Best features

Yahoo! Fantasy Football is a great way to keep current with what's going on with your league and your team when you're away from your computer. It's also good for making quick and simple changes to your roster . . .

Worst features

. . . But there are a number of things that the Yahoo! Fantasy Football Android app can't do, that you can do from the Yahoo! Fantasy Football Web site. Perhaps most importantly, you can't add players to your Watch List and you can't conduct trades with other team owners.

DivePlanner Pro
€1.00

DivePlanner Pro helps you plan multiple dives by using the official PADI RDP (Recreational Diver Planner) tables. Input the depth of your dive and your bottom time, and DivePlanner Pro indicates what your Pressure Group is. Before you head back in the water, enter your surface interval, and DivePlanner Pro displays your adjusted Pressure Group. If you also input the expected depth of your next dive, DivePlanner Pro shows you the maximum amount of time you can be underwater to stay within your no-decompression limit. If you aren't a scuba diver, don't worry if you don't understand any of this. If you *are* a diver, however, and don't understand this, then it's time for a refresher course before your next dive.

ESPN ScoreCenter
Free (ad supported)

ESPN ScoreCenter helps you keep up with the latest news and scores, and it even covers a few sports that SportsTap (also reviewed in this chapter) doesn't, such as cricket and rugby. What ESPN ScoreCenter does best is give you the information you want for just those teams and sports you care about. Choose your favorite teams, and they show up on the myTeam page, where you see the scores from the most recently played games and upcoming scheduled games.

Geocaching
$9.99 US

Putting aside the argument about whether geocaching is actually a sport, it can be a fun — and sometimes physically active — endeavor, where you use GPS to locate a hidden "treasure." With the Geocaching app, you can use your Android device to search for any of the over one million worldwide, active geocaches from the Geocaching (www.geocaching.com) library.

You can find nearby geocaches, search for them near any location you specify, or enter a specific geocache's code number (which is referred to as its "GC Code"). After you pick the geocache you want to track down, you can see all the information about it, including its description, hints, photos, and log entries from fellow geocachers who've recently searched for it.

Geocaching's best attribute, however, is its Navigate to Geocache feature. You can choose to see your present location relative to the geocache using Google Maps or with a compass view that shows the direction to the geocache and your distance from it.

Golf Channel Mobile
Free (ad supported)

With the above-par Golf Channel Mobile app, you can get the latest news of what's happening in the professional golf world, even when you're nowhere near a TV or computer. Golf Channel Mobile receives a continuous stream of golf-related news stories and updated scores from major golf tours. You can even select a player's entry from the scores to see how he or she fared in each round and on each hole. You can also read blog entries from www.thegolfchannel.com, and see video clips from the Golf Channel, including instructional videos — although I don't recommend stopping to watch a video on how to improve your swing while you're on the back nine.

Tennis Math
Free

Tennis coaches and tennis moms will love Tennis Math's capability to help them keep score during matches. In Beginner mode, all you need do is tap which player wins the point. In Intermediate mode, you can also track if the server scores an ace or faults, and if the point is won by a forced or unforced error. Professional mode lets you track additional stats for how the point was won, such as if the ball was off the net, if it was won with a backhand or forehand shot, and the type of shot (such as ground, smash, or lob).

17 Tools

Astro File Manager
$3.99 US

In my opinion, Astro File Manager should come with *every* Android device. As its name indicates, Astro File Manager helps you manage the myriad files, directories, and apps that reside on your device. Unless your device's manufacturer installed a file manager, without one on your device, you're relegated to managing your device's files from a computer that the device is attached to via a USB connection. Although this is sufficient *some* of the time, there are often times you want to manage files directly *on* the device.

The basic layout of Astro File Manager appears in the figure on the left. The contents of folders can be displayed either in list form or as thumbnail icons. You can sort the files by name, date, size, or type — in ascending or descending order. The scrolling toolbar at the top of the screen includes options such as navigating up and down directories, selecting multiple files, and performing advanced searches for files or text within files.

When you long-tap a file, you can see details about it, open it, edit it, or e-mail it. When you long-tap a directory, you can see its details and edit it, and also bookmark it and set it as the Astro File Manager's Home directory. When you select to edit a file, your options are copy, delete, move, paste, and rename. When you tap a photo, the Astro Photo Viewer launches and displays the selected photo as well as a scrollable thumbnail gallery of all the images in that folder.

Pressing the Menu button opens a window at the bottom of the screen with View, Edit, Tools, New, Bookmarks, and More button. The available Tools are Application Manager/Backup, SD Card Usage, and Process Manager. The Application Manager/Backup lets you back up, uninstall, reinstall, and launch apps.

You can only back up "public" apps. Apps that are marked as "private" (such as Life360 in the figure on the right) can't be backed up. Many paid apps are private, but you can always reinstall them from the Android Market at no additional cost, as long you use the same Google account you did when you originally purchased them.

The SD Card Usage tool shows what's on a device's removable storage and how much space it takes up. The Process Manager tool shows what apps are currently running, how much CPU and memory resources they're using, and lets you selectively "kill" running apps. It also shows running services and processes.

Best features

There are free add-on modules that allow you to browse and transfer files over network (using SAMBA) and Bluetooth connections.

Worst features

The Process Manager tool is a bit cumbersome. For managing running apps, you're better off using SystemPanel (also reviewed in this chapter).

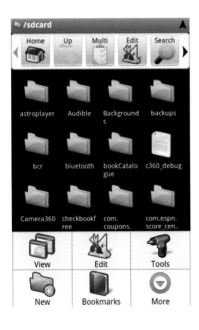

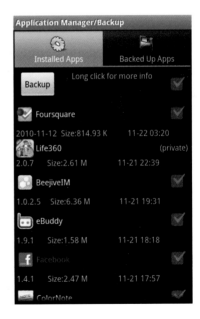

EasyTether
$9.95 US

As smart as smartphones might be, there are still things they can't do as well as computers. Tasks that require a large screen or full-size keyboard are prime examples of instances of PCs' superiority over smartphones. The trouble is, most computers don't come with built-in broadband Internet connections, so you can typically use them for Internet access only when you plug the computer into a physical network connection or get a Wi-Fi signal.

Nearly all smartphones, however, include broadband Internet access with their service subscriptions. So you can be assured you have Internet access from your smartphone virtually anywhere that isn't underground or deep in the bowels of some building.

It's for this reason that many road warriors who need Internet access from their laptops anywhere at any time add onto their smartphone service plans an additional feature that lets them use their phones as broadband Internet modems. Depending on the phone and service, a laptop can attach to a phone via a USB cable or Wi-Fi connection and piggyback on the phone's Internet connection.

This service, which is typically called tethering, often tacks on an additional $20 or $30 to your monthly mobile bill. But this isn't your only option. For just a single payment of $9.95, EasyTether will also let you tether your computer to your phone, and it shouldn't have any impact on your monthly mobile bill.

I say *"shouldn't,"* because sending and receiving a lot of data from a tethered laptop might exceed your mobile data package's monthly data allowance. After you hit your cap, you accumulate additional charges. If you frequently tether your laptop to your phone, you should use an app like 3G Watchdog (reviewed in this chapter) to keep track of your data usage. Also, EasyTether might not work with all Android phones, computers, or mobile plans, so you should first try out the free version of EasyTether to make sure it works before you purchase the paid version.

The EasyTether Setup Wizard starts by asking if you'll be tethering a Windows 7/Vista/XP/2000, Mac OS X 10.4+, or Ubuntu 10.4+ or Fedora 12+ system. Next, you must download the appropriate software that needs to be installed on the computer side of the connection. The final step is connecting your phone to your laptop via a USB cable. Your laptop should now be able to access the Internet using your phone's broadband Internet connection (the figure below shows my laptop doing exactly this).

I say *"should"* because many variables can throw a monkey wrench into the works. Most of the potential issues and their solutions are discussed on the EasyTether Web site at `www.mobile-stream.com/easytether/android_faq.html`. For example, the things I had to do to get it to work for my setup were to disable my phone's built-in tethering, turn on its USB debugging, connect the phone to my laptop in "Charge only" mode, and set the phone to stay awake while charging.

Best features

Numerous Android tethering apps exist, but this is one of the few that do *not* require root access to the phone. (Gaining root access — or "rooting" a phone — is essentially hacking a phone to get access to more of a phone's features and settings.)

Worst features

Despite your best efforts, EasyTether may not work with your setup. There's simply no way to ensure compatibility with every combination of phone, service provider, data plan, and computer.

Lookout Mobile Security
Free

For all intents and purposes, your Android device is a computer — a little tiny computer, but a computer nevertheless. And like any computer that uses an operating system and runs software, it is susceptible to the potential damage that malicious apps can cause. This "malware" can steal information stored on your device or even render your device inoperable.

And so, as with *any* computer, you *should* protect your Android device with security software (you *do* run security software, such as an anti-virus program on your computer, don't you?!?). Although security apps are still a burgeoning field for Android devices, the folks at Lookout have taken an early lead with their Android security app, Lookout Mobile Security.

Lookout Mobile Security automatically scans every new app you install to ensure that it doesn't contain any malware that can infect your device. Lookout Mobile Security can be configured to automatically scan *all* of your installed apps on a daily or weekly basis. You can also manually launch a scan of all of your installed apps at any time; the figure on the left shows the results of such a scan.

As they say in those late-night TV commercials, "But wait, there's more!" You can configure Lookout Mobile Security to back up your device's contacts and call history (if your device is a phone). This data gets saved to Lookout's online service. If you ever have to reset your phone, you can use Lookout Mobile Security to restore all of your backed-up contacts. You can't restore your call history, but you can view it — along with all sorts of other info about your device — when you log in to the Lookout Web site (www.mylookout.com).

Lookout Mobile Security can only back up your Google account-based contacts. It can't back up contacts saved to your device that are not associated with your Google account. This is a known issue and Lookout (the company) is trying to fix it.

If you ever lose your device, you can use the Lookout Web site to help locate it on a map. You can also use the site to make your device emit a loud "scream" for 60 seconds, so you can find it if you just misplaced it somewhere nearby.

Best features

Of course, Lookout Mobile Security's best features aren't free, but can be accessed only by subscribing to Lookout's Premium service ($2.99 per month or $29.99 per year). With a Premium subscription (available as a free 30-day trial), you can also back up and restore photos saved on your device. Speaking of restores, a Premium subscription also lets you restore your data to a *different* device, should your current device ever be lost, stolen, damaged, or upgraded. A Premium subscription also means that if your device goes missing, you can remotely lock it and even remotely wipe all of your personal data from it.

A Premium subscription also adds a Privacy Advisor tool, which identifies the installed apps that can access your location, identity, and saved text messages. The figure on the right shows some of the apps installed on my device that can access text messages.

Worst features

Backing up and restoring contacts and photos is helpful, but this feature would be more useful if it also backed up and restored text messages, documents, videos, music, and other similar files. For backing up your Android device, MyBackup Pro (also reviewed in this chapter) is a better choice.

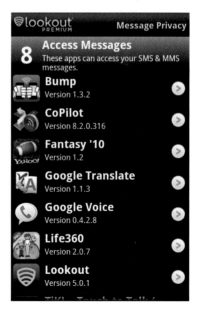

 **Tasker**
£3.99

Tasker is one the most powerful tools for Android devices I've ever seen. Tasker lets you program your device to perform particular actions or behave in certain ways, depending on any number of variables, such as the time of day, the device's specific location, or when a particular app is running. The extent to which you can program Tasker is limited only by your imagination and your ability to grasp all of the app's nuances — programmed tasks can range from simple to mind-boggling.

For each set of actions you program, you first create a Profile, such as the two I created in the figure on the left: "Bat Status When No Power Source," and "Leave Home Sound Level." A Profile is merely a container within which the actions you program reside.

After you create a Profile, the next step is to add a Context. A Context is the set of conditions that trigger the desired actions. Just some of the many possible Contexts you can choose from are if a specific app is running, if a headset is plugged in, and if a particular button is pushed. You can add multiple Contexts to a Profile to set a unique set of conditions. In my "Leave Home Sound Level" Profile, I set up a single Context that triggers whenever my device is no longer near my home Wi-Fi router.

The final step is to program the Task you want to take place when the Contexts are triggered (you can add multiple actions to a Task). Choose from 15 categories of possible actions, which include over 180 actions. See the figure on the right for the different categories. In my "Leave Home Sound Level" Profile, I have five actions in the Task, which set specific levels for my device's alarm, media, ringer, in-call, and system volume levels.

 You can even use variables and loops for your Tasks. The best way to learn about the many things you can do with Tasker is to take the online tour of the app at `tasker.dinglisch.net/tour.html` and to see the sample Profiles at `tasker.wikidot.com/profile-index`.

My "Leave Home Sound Level" Profile automatically sets my device's different volume levels when the device is away from my Wi-Fi router at home. I do this so that when I leave the house (and I'm therefore away from my Wi-Fi router), I know that all of my device's different volume levels will be set loud enough for me to hear them, despite what I might have had them set at when I was at home. The other Profile I created automatically pops up a window with the device's remaining battery power whenever I disconnect it from the charger or my computer.

Best features

Once you master Tasker, there is no limit to the tasks you can automate.

Worst features

Tasker can be a very challenging app to figure out — especially if you are not technically minded.

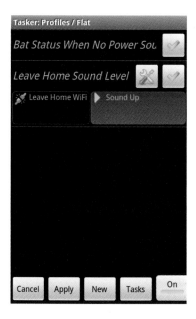

Vlingo: Words to Action
Free

Vlingo: Words to Action does exactly what its name implies . . . Speak a command and the app does what you tell it to. It can't walk the dog or make dinner, but it can *find* a dog walker and *text* your friend to *tell* her that you're running late for your dinner date.

Vlingo: Words to Action is a voice command app that accesses functions on your device that are typically relegated to keyboard input. Instead, just tap the Tap & Speak button (see the figure on the left), speak a command, and then tap the Done button. Assuming that Vlingo: Words to Action understands what you said — and I've had excellent luck with it understanding my spoken words — it admirably performs the task or fetches the requested information. Some things you can do with Vlingo: Words to Action are:

- **Make a phone call:** Say "call Barack Obama at work," and Vlingo: Words to Action dials the number from your contacts. Say "call Conan O'Brien," and a window opens with all the relevant names and number matches from your contacts. Say "call pizza" and you'll see a list of nearby pizza-related businesses.

- **Send text messages:** Say "Send text to Lady Gaga, How are you, question mark," and Vlingo: Words to Action composes and addresses the message. All you need do is tap the Send button.

- **Search:** Say "movie times," and Google searches results for local movie theaters. In fact, you can pretty much say anything that doesn't fit into any of these categories and Vlingo: Words to Action treats it as a Google search.

- **Open apps:** Say "launch calendar," and Vlingo: Words to Action opens the Calendar app.

    Vlingo: Words to Action can open apps that come standard with Android devices, but it can't open third-party apps you install. If you were to say "launch Angry Birds," you'd wind up just seeing Google search results for the text, "launch angry birds."

- **Update social networking status:** Say "Twitter, look ma, no hands, exclamation mark," and your Twitter client opens with the message ready for you tap the Update button. Vlingo: Words to Action can also send Facebook and Foursquare status updates.

Best features

The Vlingo InCar Beta feature (see the figure on the right) takes the app a step further by making Vlingo: Words to Action a truly hands-free experience. Just say "hey Vlingo," and a voice chimes in, asking "what would you like to do?" State what you'd like to do or search for — without having to tap any buttons — and Vlingo: Words to Action completes the task. You can even set the Vlingo InCar Beta to read incoming texts and e-mails to you, as they arrive.

Even being completely hands-free doesn't guarantee that you still won't get distracted. If you use the Vlingo InCar Beta feature while driving, do so with extreme caution.

Worst features

If you use Vlingo: Words to Action in a moving vehicle, in all likelihood you're going to need to use a Bluetooth headset. Otherwise, the road noise in the background may prevent your device's microphone from hearing you clearly.

3G Watchdog
Free

Many broadband data plans have monthly caps on just how much data you're allowed to send and receive. Go over the limit and you're charged for extra data usage. Even if you have an "unlimited" plan, read the fine print — your plan might not be as unlimited as you think it is. A great way to keep an eye on your mobile data consumption is to use 3G Watchdog, which sits in the background, monitoring your received and transmitted data usage. It places a green icon in your device's notification bar, telling you that you *aren't* near your data cap. The icon turns orange when you approach the cap, and red when you go over.

3G Watchdog isn't smart enough to know what your specific data plan's limit is, so you need to plug this information into the app's settings.

MyBackup Pro
$4.99 US

Unless you "root" your device, it's virtually impossible to back up every single app, file, and setting on it. (When you root an Android device, you essentially hack it to expose features that the device manufacturer and service providers would prefer you didn't have access to). MyBackup Pro comes as close as it gets to backing up as much as is possible from a non-rooted device.

MyBackup Pro can back up a device's applications, contacts, call log, bookmarks, SMS and MMS messages, system settings, Android Home, alarms, dictionary, and calendar. You can choose to back up to your device's SD Card or to the MyBackup online service. You can restore backed-up data to the same device or a new device.

MyBackup Pro can't back up any apps that are designated as "private." MyBackup Pro also doesn't back up photos, videos, or music files.

SwiftKey Keyboard
$3.99 US

If you think all onscreen keyboards are created equal, you're in for a very pleasant surprise with SwiftKey Keyboard — especially when compared against the default onscreen keyboard that came with your device. SwiftKey Keyboard is an "intelligent" keyboard that predicts what words you're typing based on just the first few letters and also has an uncanny capability to even know when you misspell a word. The more you use it, the better it gets at predicting words — it learns from what you write over time. SwiftKey Keyboard even builds a voice-to-text module into the keyboard so that you can speak the text you want to input.

 ## SystemPanel App / Task Manager
$2.99 US

SystemPanel App / Task Manager is another app that should come standard with every Android device. It provides a wealth of information about the device, how the device's resources (such as CPU, memory, and storage) are used, and shows details about running and installed apps.

SystemPanel App / Task Manager lets you install and uninstall apps, as well as create multiple backup copies of different versions of your apps. You can also use SystemPanel App / Task Manager to terminate running apps or to kill all currently running tasks. If you choose to kill all the running tasks, SystemPanel App / Task Manager lets you create an exceptions list for any apps that you want to keep running while everything else stops.

 ## Uninstaller Pro
Free (ad supported)

Uninstaller Pro is a simple app with the single-minded purpose of quickly uninstalling apps from Android devices. And it performs this task admirably with features such as searching for apps by name, and the capability to sort the list of installed apps by name, size, or date installed (all in ascending or descending order). My favorite feature, however, is the capability to select multiple apps and perform batch uninstalls. As I installed and uninstalled *hundreds* of apps to evaluate for this book, Uninstaller Pro quickly became my best friend.

18 Travel and Navigation

Top Ten Apps

▶ Car Finder AR

▶ CoPilot Live – North America

▶ Google Maps

▶ Kayak Flight and Hotel Search

▶ Trip Journal

 Car Finder AR

€2.40

If you regularly drive a car, chances are that at one time or another you've forgotten where you parked it. Or perhaps you lost your car somewhere in the massive parking lot of your local mega-mall. Unfortunately, you can't yell out its name, hoping that it will answer back with an emphatic, "I'm over here!" (Pressing the door-lock button on the remote sometimes works, however, if you're reasonably close to your car.) No, it's up to you to find it.

If you do this more often than you'd like to admit, you need Car Finder AR. Of course, you have to *remember* to use Car Finder AR; assuming you do, it will steer you straight to your car every time.

After you park your car and are ready to venture forth, launch the Car Finder AR app, which displays a map of your current location. If you prefer, you can use a satellite view instead. Tap your device's Menu button, and then tap the Save Location button to record your car's location. An icon representing your car now appears on the map. If you tap the icon, a menu pops up with a few options, such as share the location via e-mail, texting, or social networking; write a note for yourself; or set an alarm. The alarm is helpful when you need a reminder to throw a few more quarters into a parking meter.

 Car Finder AR provides two other ways to save the location where you parked: Set it to save the location by shaking your device, or if your car has Bluetooth, set Car Finder AR to automatically save the location when it detects that your device has disconnected from your car's Bluetooth. (This requires also installing the free Car Finder AR Bluetooth Plug-in.)

Car Finder AR lets you save up to three locations. You don't have to use each location for a different car, however. One can be where you parked, one can be a gas station you passed that had cheap gas, and the third could be a hard-to-find restaurant you want to remember.

When it's time to find your car, you see two icons on the map. One is your car, and the other is your present location. Now it's just a question of navigating your way back to where your car is parked.

You can also use a nifty Radar view to find your car. Your car appears as a dot on a radar screen. As you turn around, the dot moves, showing the direction to your car. As you move closer to your car, the dot moves closer to the center of the radar screen.

Best features

The "AR" in the app's name refers to augmented reality, where information displays on top of a live view from your device's camera. Using AR View, a triangle pointing toward your car is superimposed over what your camera sees. As you move, the arrow adjusts accordingly. AR View also displays the distance to your car.

Worst features

Car Finder AR uses GPS, which works only as long as your device has a reasonably clear view of the sky. Car Finder AR won't work in underground garages.

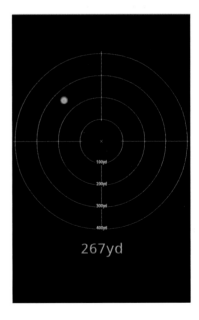

CoPilot Live – North America
$19.99 US

It wasn't that long ago that I had to keep a full complement of maps in my car's glove compartment. Those maps really came in handy when I made a wrong turn or got lost. (Mostly because I stubbornly refused to ask for directions.) More recently, the ubiquitous nature of dedicated GPS navigation devices has pretty much relegated paper maps to the status of curious antiques. Now with inexpensive GPS navigation apps, such as CoPilot Live – North America, even GPS devices are becoming superfluous.

 CoPilot Live is available in versions for different locations, such as Australia, Europe, South Africa, and the U.K. and Ireland. If you find CoPilot Live – North America's price tag too steep and you don't need maps of Canada, CoPilot Live USA's $4.99 cost might be a much better bargain.

At its core, CoPilot Live delivers clearly spoken, GPS-guided, turn-by-turn directions. Not only does it say the street names (with the occasional mispronunciation), but it guides you to the correct lane when needed and even matches what you see on the road signs. If you make a wrong turn, CoPilot Live instantly recalculates the route to get you back on track. You can set when CoPilot Live alerts you to upcoming turns — the options are 2 miles out, 1 mile away, .3 mile ahead of time, and at the turn. You can choose some or all of those options, and you can even customize the "at turn" setting to chime in when you're anywhere between 150 and 400 yards away.

To enter a destination, type in an address, enter an intersection, or pick it on a map. You can also choose a destination from recent or favorite locations, which can include your home and work. You can even choose from CoPilot Live's massive Point-of-Interest database, which has locations such as gas stations, restaurants, and banks. If you're planning a long trip, you can input multiple stops. Unfortunately, the most convenient way of inputting destinations — simply picking them from your device's contacts — isn't currently supported. Hopefully, it'll be added to the app at some point (perhaps even by the time you read this).

While you should keep your eyes on the road while driving, CoPilot Live also includes 2D and 3D map views with the option of placing north or the direction you are heading at the top of the screen. You can also call up an itinerary that lists every turn of your trip. The map also shows how far you are from the next turn and includes an arrow that points in the direction the turn will be. A customizable Info Bar sits on the bottom of the screen, where you can choose to display data such as your estimated time of arrival (ETA), your current speed, and the name of the road you are on.

Best features

CoPilot Live includes a set of features that it calls "Live Services," which lets you do things like share your current location with others or see a five-day weather forecast for your present location. You can also get live traffic updates where CoPilot Live will recalculate your route to help you avoid an incident. The ActiveTraffic service sub-scription costs $9.99 per year.

Worst features

Because CoPilot Live is designed to work even when you don't have a data connection, you must store all of the app's map data on your device. CoPilot Live – North America's data files require around 1.8GB of space on your device's SD card.

Google Maps
Free

As with all things Google, the question is not what can Google Maps do, but what can't it do? The fact that you can see maps and satellite views of virtually any part of our planet is just the tip of the iceberg. Here, I skate through several of Google Maps' features, but note that I just scratch the surface of its capabilities, and the app is frequently updated with new features.

When you launch Google Maps, it tries to get a fix on your location and places a blue arrowhead on the map where it thinks you are. Since GPS positioning is not always precise, a transparent blue circle that represents the range of accuracy of the current GPS fix surrounds the arrowhead — the smaller the circle, the more accurate the location.

Tap and hold any place on the map, and a bubble appears that provides that location's address and nearby businesses. Tap the bubble to open a new screen that gives you options for finding out "What's nearby?," a Street View of that location (such as the figure on the left, which shows Wiley headquarters in Hoboken, NJ), and even navigation or directions there from your current location. The Google Maps Navigation module provides GPS-guided, spoken, turn-by-turn, driving or walking directions. You can also choose to see just written directions — and not just for driving and walking — but also for biking or mass transit. Google Maps even provides relevant train and bus schedules.

If you tap the "What's nearby?" prompt and choose one of the listings — such as a restaurant — a screen appears that provides detailed information about that business. Here you find things like user reviews, business hours, and a link to the business's Web site. Tap the phone icon to launch your device's phone app (assuming your Android device is a phone) to call the business.

Another way to find out what's nearby is to tap the Places icon at the top of the screen — the upside-down teardrop-shaped icon in the figure on the right. The Places module launches, which lets you choose from categories such as Bars, Attractions, and ATMs. You can add your own custom categories as well, such as Pizza or Pharmacies.

If you're wondering what those red, yellow, and green lines are in the figure on the right, they're a real-time indication what traffic was like when I took the screenshot. Traffic is just one of the many Layers of additional data in Google Maps. Some other Layer options are Terrain, Transit Lines, Buzz, and Latitude.

Buzz is a social networking feature where people can publicly post information and pictures about locations, such as drink specials at a bar, something cool they saw, or even just their own personal ramblings. When someone posts a Buzz about a location, a little cartoon speech balloon appears at that spot in Google Maps. Tap the balloon to read the Buzz.

Latitude is another social networking feature. It lets you share your current location with your friends and see exactly where they are. Unlike Buzz, Latitude is not broadcast for the world to see. Only those people to whom you grant permission can see your whereabouts.

Best features

You aren't limited to searching just what you see on the screen. Type anything you are looking for into the search bar, and Google Maps will locate it, no matter where it is in the world.

Worst features

Unlike CoPilot Live or NAVIGON MobileNavigator (which are both reviewed in this chapter), Google Maps requires an active data connection (Wi-Fi, Edge, 3G, or 4G) in order to access any of this information. If your device doesn't have a data connection, Google Maps displays a blank screen.

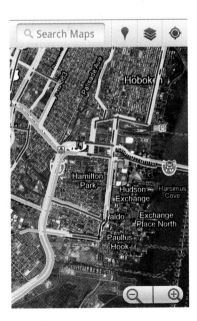

Kayak Flight and Hotel Search

Free (ad supported)

Short of using a travel agent for your next vacation or business trip, Kayak Flight and Hotel Search might be your best bet for finding the best options and cheapest rates for wherever you plan to go. Kayak Flight and Hotel Search is a travel search engine that collects data from hundreds of sites — including airlines, hotels, travel agencies, and discount travel-booking sites.

The figure on the left shows Kayak Flight and Hotel Search's main screen, which lets you search for flights, hotels, and rental cars. When you search for flights, input where you're flying from, where you're going, your departure and return dates, preferred cabin class (economy, premium, business, or first class), and specify the number of travelers. You can also add multi-city destinations, choose if you're looking for one-way fares, and only want to consider nonstop flights.

If you have some wiggle room with your travel dates, select the "Flex Days" option, which will also look for cheaper fares for flights that are within a few days of your departure and return dates. Select the "Nearby Location" option to see if there are better flight options close by.

After you enter all your search criteria, tap the Search button. It might take a minute or two, but soon you'll see a results screen that looks something like the figure on the right. The search results appear in a long list of flights that meet your requirements. At the top of the page, you can choose to see flights sorted by those that are cheapest, shortest, or leaving the soonest. At the bottom of the page, you can filter results by criteria such as the number of stops, specific airlines, or price range.

Scroll through the list until you find a good candidate and select it. This takes you to a summary screen of the flight details, including layover information and even how many seats are still available. If you like what you see, tap the Book button at the top of the page. At this point, a window pops up with options for where you can purchase your tickets, such as Orbitz or Vayama. Tap one of these options and your device's Web browser launches, taking you to the site you picked. (Kayak Flight and Hotel Search does not actually book tickets. It finds the best deals and then passes you off to another company to seal the deal.)

Search for hotels and rental cars much the same way. When you search for a hotel or car, the search automatically uses the same destination and dates you provided when you looked for flights. Adjust these as needed.

Kayak Flight and Hotel Search can do plenty more to help you book your trip. It provides Web site links and phone numbers for every airline you can think of — and many that you've probably never heard of. You can also look up fees that each airline charges, such as for checked bags, meals, or unaccompanied minors service. After you book your reservations, forward the confirmation e-mails to a special e-mail address, and your trip information will automatically show up in the app and appear in your calendar (this requires signing up for a free account).

Best features

Kayak Flight and Hotel Search provides the most exhaustive travel search results I've ever seen.

Worst features

You can't book complete vacation packages or cruises, or look up travel deals with Kayak Flight and Hotel Search. These are things you *can* do, however, on the Web site, www.kayak.com.

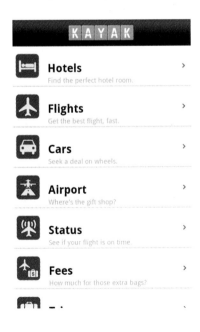

Trip Journal
€2.99

The days of making your friends and family sit through slideshows of your vacations may be long over, but there are still ways to share your travel memories with everyone. And I don't mean just uploading a bunch of holiday snaps to your Flickr account. Instead, with Trip Journal, folks can follow your adventures as fun, interactive, multi-media explorations.

The first step in using Trip Journal is that you actually have to go somewhere. Preferably someplace interesting. Whenever you stop at a noteworthy location, launch Trip Journal and create a waypoint. A waypoint marks the specific GPS coordinates of your current location. Next, take photos and videos using your device's camera, and they'll be associated with that waypoint. You can also add photos and videos that are already saved in your device's memory. You can add notes that will be associated with the waypoint, too. If you don't have time to stop and make entries, you can always go back into Trip Journal later and make whatever edits and additions you see fit.

At any point, you can call up a map view, which shows your current location on Google Maps (you can select either a map or satellite view). While looking at the map, you can add new waypoints, as well as see all your previously recorded waypoints from your trip. From this page, you can also send out a Tweet that includes a link to your present location on Google Maps.

If you need a little extra help navigating while you're getting around, Trip Journal includes a compass view that helps point you back in the right direction. This page also displays some statistics from your trip, such as the total distance you've covered, your average speed, and how long you've been traveling.

 If you use the Track Route option, Trip Journal continuously records your GPS coordinates, tracking the precise route you take.

Best features

The real power of Trip Journal kicks in when you're ready to share your journey with everyone who wasn't lucky enough to be there with you. You can do this after you return from your trip, or even while you're still traveling.

The Google Earth export option takes all your GPS tracks, waypoints, and associated media and notes, and wraps it all up into a KMZ (Keyhole Markup Language-Zipped) file that you can then e-mail to whomever you want. Recipients open the KMZ file in Google Earth, with which they can follow your trip chronologically and see your photos, videos, and notes pop up at each waypoint.

You can also export your trip to Facebook to share with your friends. They need to install the free Trip Journal Facebook application in order to view it. If you want to post just the photos from your travels, Trip Journal lets you export them directly to Picasa and Flickr. Finally, if you are a GPS fanatic, you can also export your GPS tracks and way-points as a GPX (GPS eXchange Format) file that can be read by many GPS mapping applications.

Worst features

It takes time to figure everything out about Trip Journal. Get up to speed with the app well *before* you leave for your trip.

FlightTrack

$4.99 US

FlightTrack is a must-have app for frequent flyers. Enter your domestic and international flights into FlightTrack, and it delivers real-time updates as soon as there are changes to the status of any of your flights. FightTrack provides terminal, gate, and baggage information. It also displays airport information (such as FAA delays and closures) and weather forecasts. You can see in-air flights displayed on a map, and you can even share your flight information with others via e-mail, texting, or social networking. If your flight is delayed or canceled, tap the Find Alternate selection to see what your flight options might be.

GasBuddy – Find Cheap Gas

Free

One of the great quests that nearly every frequent driver faces is to find the cheapest gas available. It might only be a few cents less per gallon than the station down the block, but it adds up as the miles pile on. Luckily, with Gas Buddy – Find Cheap Gas in your arsenal, you needn't drive those extra miles looking for the lowest price at the pump. You can search by city or zip code, or simply tap the Find Gas Near Me button to see what's close by. You can sort the results by price or distance, or display the prices on a map. You can see prices for Regular, Midgrade, Premium, and Diesel.

All the gas prices are submitted by users. If you use Gas Buddy – Find Cheap Gas, please return the favor and use the app to report the prices you see at the gas stations you frequent.

NAVIGON MobileNavigator USA

€45.25

NAVIGON MobileNavigator USA is a robust, GPS-guided navigation app that provides spoken, turn-by-turn directions. It shares many similarities with CoPilot Live (also reviewed in this chapter), such as its extensive map data and points-of-interest database (which together eat up 1.5GB of space on your device's SD card), and the capability to instantly recalculate your route.

NAVIGON MobileNavigator has a few features that CoPilot Live doesn't — most notably, it *can* access your device's contacts. NAVIGON MobileNavigator even includes an augmented-reality feature, Reality Scanner, where information about nearby businesses appears over a live image of what your device's camera sees. Like CoPilot Live, NAVIGON MobileNavigator offers live traffic updates. Unlike CoPilot Live, however, there's no additional cost for this service. It mostly comes to personal preference, but I find NAVIGON MobileNavigator isn't as easy to use as CoPilot Live. CoPilot Live is also less expensive.

 # Ride Hopper Full
$0.99 US

One of the biggest challenges with theme parks is trying to not spend all your time waiting in line. You want to get in as many rides as possible. With more than 4,300 rides at 260-plus theme parks in its database, you can get up-to-the-minute wait times for all the rides at the park you're visiting. If a ride's wait time is too long for you, set Ride Hopper Full to alert you when the wait time is more reasonable (you can set the alerts between no-wait and 120 minutes). You can also add specific rides to a Favorites list, making it easier to check on only the rides that interest you.

Ride Hopper Full depends on the community of its users to report the ride wait times — this means you too!

 # Transport Maps 1.6
Free

If you suddenly find yourself in need of a public transportation map for a major metropolitan area almost anywhere in the world (such as Kuala Lumpur, Brussels, or Seattle), chances are you can download and view it with Transport Maps. Maps get added to the growing database by users who upload them to the Transport Maps submission Web site (`transportmaps.free.fr`). The maps are large JPG files with which you can zoom and pan. There aren't any additional bells and whistles, such as links to station or fare information, but the maps are easy to read and will help get you where you need to go in a jiffy.

19 Utilities

Dropbox
Free

Dropbox lets you automatically sync files between multiple systems, access files remotely from a Web browser, and share files with other people. Some folks even use Dropbox to back up their important files online. Although Dropbox has mostly been the mainstay of Windows, Mac, and Linux computer users, the Dropbox Android app (along with versions for the iPhone, iPad, and Blackberry devices) makes it super easy to access your files from your mobile device as well.

Before I dive into the Android app version of Dropbox, I need to explain how the computer version of Dropbox works. With the free Dropbox software running (downloadable from www.dropbox.com), any file you copy into the Dropbox folder on that system's hard drive automatically copies to your online Dropbox account. Conversely, any files that you place into your online Dropbox account (such as from another computer or from your Android device) automatically download to your system's Dropbox folder — thus keeping your files in sync across every computer that's running the Dropbox software.

The Dropbox Android app has complete access to all of the files that are synced to your online Dropbox account. What the Android version *doesn't* do, however, is automatically copy files down from your online Dropbox account to the device's SD Card. In all likelihood, you don't need access to *all* of those files on your device, and they could very quickly fill up the SD Card.

Instead, use the Dropbox Android app to browse the files that are stored in your online Dropbox account (see the figure on the left). When you want to access a file, simply tap it and it automatically downloads to your device — and if an associated app is installed, the file automatically opens in the app. You can also long-tap a file for options to download and open it, download it without opening it, share the file with someone, or delete it.

You can upload files from your device to your online Dropbox account using the Dropbox app (see the figure on the right), but there is an easier way to this: Apps that let you browse files stored on your device (such as music or video players or file managers) usually include a Send or Share feature that lets you send files via numerous options, such as with e-mail or posting on Facebook. After you install and configure Dropbox on your device, sending to your online Dropbox account is added to this list.

Best features

If your device has a camera and a dedicated camera button, you can automatically send photos directly your online Dropbox account. With Dropbox open on the screen, press your device's Camera button to launch the camera app. When you shoot your picture, the photo saves to your device's storage as normal and automatically uploads to your online Dropbox account.

Worst features

A free Dropbox account provides only 2GB of storage. Additional online storage costs $9.99 per month for 50GB, or $19.99 per month for 100GB.

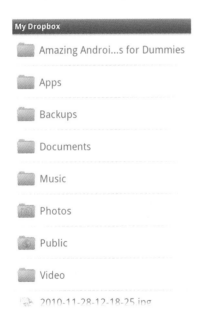

MyPhoneExplorer Client
Free

MyPhoneExplorer is a powerful Windows program that lets you manage your Android device and sync data and files between your device and computer. To use it, you must first install the MyPhoneExplorer Client app onto your Android device and then launch the app. On your Windows system, you have to install and run the free MyPhoneExplorer software (downloadable from `www.fjsoft.at`). With the app and the software running, the MyPhoneExplorer software communicates with your device via either a USB or Wi-Fi connection (select File and then Connect from the MyPhoneExplorer software's menu bar).

 I found the Wi-Fi connection to be much easier to use than USB; the USB connection requires you to install special drivers on your computer and set your device to USB debugging mode.

With the MyPhoneExplorer Windows software connected to your device, you can sync your contacts and calendars between your device and your computer. If you use multiple accounts on your device, you can set which of those accounts you want to sync with your system from the MyPhoneExplorer Android app's settings. You can also select which account on your device that you want new contacts and calendar entries from your computer to sync to.

On the Windows side, you can sync your device's contacts and calendars to MyPhoneExplorer's built-in phonebook, your Google account, or apps such as Outlook, Lotus Notes, or Thunderbird. If your Android device is a phone, you can also sync your phone's call log and SMS text messages to the MyPhoneExplorer software.

When viewing the call log from the MyPhoneExplorer software, you can select an entry to have your phone make a call or send a text message to the selected number. You can also add the number to the phonebook and do a reverse search (to find out the name associated with the number using public records on the Internet).

When looking at your text messages, you can have your phone send a new text message, forward the text to a different number, or call the number. You can also copy or move the message to the MyPhoneExplorer software's archive, as well as print or delete the message.

Best features

I already sync my contacts and calendar using my Google account, so I don't use those features of MyPhoneExplorer. Instead, I use MyPhoneExplorer to see which apps and files are on my device's internal and removable storage and to easily copy files between my device and my computer.

You can create custom sync jobs that sync files between designated folders on your device and computer. An Applications window enables you to see which apps are installed on your device, launch an app, download an app from your device to your computer, install an app onto your device from your computer, and delete an app from the device.

Hidden in the MyPhoneExplorer Windows software's settings (on the Multi-sync tab) is an option to automatically sync the photos stored on your device to your computer.

Worst features

The MyPhoneExplorer software lacks a Mac version.

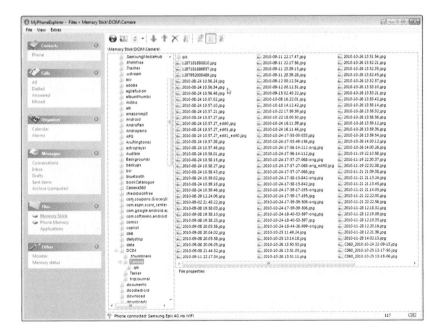

Remote Desktop Client
$24.95 US

Geek alert: This app requires some networking know-how.

One of the trusty tools in a computer system administrator's arsenal is the Remote Desktop Protocol (RDP), which has been built into some versions of the Windows operating system as far back as Windows XP. By using RDP software on a remote system over the Internet, an admin can log into a Windows system or server and take over nearly full control of the system. (When you log in to a system using RDP, you log into that system's RDP Server service. I refer to the system that's being logged into as the server.)

You're not always going to be in front of a computer when disaster strikes. When an emergency login is required and all you've got with you is your Android device, it's time to fire up the Remote Desktop Client app and remotely access the system in need.

The Remote Desktop Client has a pretty basic interface. On the main screen, you add entries for all the servers you plan on remotely accessing. Each server listing has a General tab and an Advanced tab. In many cases, all you need to provide to gain access to the server are the address of the server, a username, and password (see the figure on the left). Additional settings on the General tab include providing a domain name and setting the screen resolution and display color depth.

The Advanced tab includes settings for which security layer to use (RDP, negotiate, or SSL), where the server's sound should play (no sound, on the server, or on your device), and enables copying text between the server and your device. You can also specify a program to run and a folder to start in when the RDP session starts on the server.

After an RDP connection is established, the server's desktop appears on your device's screen. You can view it in both landscape and portrait modes. Pinch to zoom or use the optional zoom controls (see the figure on the right). By default, you navigate around the desktop as though your device's screen is a touchpad. (You can change this setting if you want, but touchpad mode gives you the most precise control of the pointer.)

Single-tap for a left mouse click, double-tap for a left mouse double-click, and tap and hold for a right mouse click. From the Menu, you can call up the Android keyboard for text entry or a special set of Windows menu keys, such as Esc, Ctrl, and PgDn.

To access a system that's on the same local area network (LAN), logging in should be as simple as providing the local IP address of the system and giving a proper username and password. If you connect to a system from the Internet, however, you likely need to take a few extra steps first, such as setting up a Dynamic DNS (DDNS) service and forwarding the appropriate ports on your router. If these concepts seem alien to you, check out the step-by-step configuration guide for using Remote Desktop Client over an Internet connection at www.xtralogic.com/rdc_cfg_guide.shtml.

Best features

Remote Desktop Client includes a feature that lets your device's SD Card show up as a disk on the server, making it easy to copy files between the server and your device.

Worst features

Remote Desktop Client only works with some versions of Windows. If your computer is running Windows 7 Home Premium or it's a Mac, you won't be able to access it remotely using Remote Desktop Client from your device.

Remote VNC Pro
$5.98 US

Geek alert: This app requires some networking know-how.

When it comes to remotely logging into a computer to gain control over the display and keyboard and mouse input, VNC (Virtual Network Computing) is one of the more popular methods. Its popularity has largely to do with the fact that you can run VNC software on just about any computer, making VNC a solid choice when the systems you are logging in from and to are running different operating systems. Another popular but more limited method, RDP (Remote Desktop Protocol), can be used only to log into systems running specific versions of the Windows operating system — such as the Remote Desktop Client app (also reviewed in this chapter).

My primary computer is a Mac, and when I want to remotely access it over the Internet from an Android device, I use the Remote VNC Pro app. (A VNC server is built into the Mac operating system, but there are plenty of VNC server software options available for virtually all operating systems.) Much like Remote Desktop Client, Remote VNC Pro needs just a few bits of information to set up a remote connection: the host's address, VNC port, and VNC password.

But also like the Remote Desktop Client, to remotely connect to a system over the Internet with Remote VNC Pro requires a little networking black magic to get things working. Unless the system you are logging into has a static IP address and isn't behind a router, use a Dynamic DNS (DDNS) service. And if the system is connected to a router, you need to forward the requisite ports on your router to the system you want to log into. For a good walk-through on how to set all this up, take a gander at www.dyndns.com/support/kb/tightvnc_quick_guide.html.

After you get it all working and you're remotely connected to your computer, your system's display appears on your device's screen. Pinch or unpinch to zoom in and out, or use the onscreen zoom controls. Flick to move around the display, tap to left-click or move the cursor, and tap and drag to make selections, such as selecting text from a document. Speaking of selecting text, you can copy text between the remotely connected system and your Android device. Tap and hold to right-click. You can opt instead to use the Touchpad mode, which as its name implies, treats your device's touchscreen as a touchpad mouse for scrolling around the remotely connected system's screen. You can view the remote connection in both landscape and portrait modes.

Remote VNC Pro includes a number of predefined "keys" you can send to the remote system with just the tap of a button, such as Control-Alt-Delete, Alt-Tab, and F1. You can also add your own customizable keys, with up to four key presses per key, such as Option-Shift-Command-V.

Best features

Remote VNC Pro includes an ingenious onscreen mouse mode that makes it super easy to select text and do left and right mouse clicks (see the figure below). Just drag the onscreen mouse and tap the mouse buttons as though you were using a real computer mouse.

Worst features

Unlike the Remote Desktop Client app, Remote VNC Pro doesn't let you copy files between the remotely connected system and your device. Remote VNC Pro also can't play the audio from your computer.

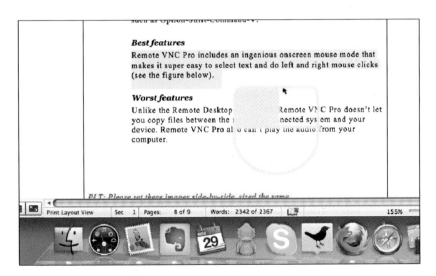

WebSharing File/ Media Sync
$2.99 US

If you read the reviews of the other apps in this chapter, then no doubt you realize that many of these apps allow you to copy files on and off your Android device, among other things. Well, here's yet another app that gives you access to the files stored on your device's storage. The difference with WebSharing File/Media Sync, however, is that its *sole purpose* is to act as a conduit to your device's files over a wireless connection. It's also easy to use (no networking knowledge required) and has an elegant user interface.

Setting up WebSharing File/Media Sync is ridiculously easy. In fact, in most situations, no setup is required! Just fire up the app and tap the Start button, and it's ready to go. "WebSharing is active" shows on the screen, plus an address you type into your computer's browser, and a password.

Now just launch a Web browser on your computer and point it at the address that appears on the WebSharing File/Media Sync screen. A Welcome screen in your browser asks for the password. Type in the password and the next screen should look something like the following figure, which shows the files and folders on the device's removable storage.

In order to connect your computer to your device with WebSharing File/Media Sync, your system and device need to be on the same local network, such as both connected to the same Wi-Fi router. Alternatively, if your Android device is a phone, you can connect your computer to it using the phone's broadband data connection. You need to turn the Cellular access option on in the Network settings section of WebSharing File/Media Sync's settings. Note that connecting via a data connection will be much slower than over a Wi-Fi connection, and it doesn't work with all service providers.

In the Web browser on your computer, you can view your device's files as icons or as a list. Double-click a folder to open it and see its contents. You can select individual files or folders or multiple files and folders. After you make your selection, you can download the selected items, cut them (in order to paste them elsewhere), copy them, or delete them. If you download more than one item at a time, all the files will automatically be combined into a single zip file. You can also upload single or multiple files to your device, paste files you've cut, and rename files.

The WebSharing File/Media Sync browser interface also has Music, Photos, and Videos tabs, which access the media files stored on your device. On these pages, you can listen to music, see photos, and watch videos that reside on the device without having to first copy them off. You can also download media files from these pages to your computer (the music page also lets you upload music files to your device).

Best features

You can allow "guests" to have limited access to the files on your device. You can select if guests have access to your device's files, music, photos, and videos; and you can choose to give them file and music upload privileges as well.

WebSharing File/Media Sync includes a WebDAV feature that lets you mount your device as a disk, so that you can treat your device's storage as though it's an external hard drive connected to your computer. This feature is marked as a beta, but it worked without a hitch for me.

Worst features

I'm just nit-picking here, but it would great if you could also upload folders.

Gmote 2.0
Free

Gmote enables you to use your Android device as a Wi-Fi remote control for watching movies and listening to music on your computer. After you install, launch, and configure the free Gmote server software (downloadable from www.gmote.org/server) on your Windows, Mac, or Linux computer, just fire up the Gmote app on your device and wirelessly connect it to the Gmote server on the computer.

You can browse the media folders, select movies to watch, and music to play on your computer. For some file types, you can even stream media from your computer to your device. Gmote also includes a cool feature that lets you use your device's touchscreen as a remote touchpad interface for your computer for controlling your computer's mouse pointer and left and right mouse clicks.

LastPass for Dolphin HD *Prem.
Free (subscription required)

LastPass for Dolphin HD *Prem. is a password manager add-in for the Dolphin Browser HD (my favorite Android Web browser, which I review in Chapter 3). With this add-in, you never have to remember all the usernames and passwords you use to log in to the different sites you frequent. Instead, LastPass for Dolphin HD *Prem. fills it in for you. All you have to remember is your LastPass username and master password, as all your disparate log-in credentials are securely stored in the online LastPass vault (www.lastpass.com). You can also store profile information, such as your name, address, and credit card numbers, and use LastPass for Dolphin HD *Prem. to auto-fill on sites that request such information.

Unfortunately, you can't add *new* log-in credentials to your LastPass vault with LastPass for Dolphin HD *Prem. — you can only access *existing* usernames and passwords from your LastPass vault. The assumption here is that you're also using LastPass on your computer, which is where you initially create your username and password entries when you log into sites. If you want to save new log-in credentials to your LastPass vault from your Android device, you can do so using the free LastPass for Premium Customers app Web browser. Note that both LastPass for Dolphin HD *Prem. and LastPass for Premium Customers require a LastPass Premium account, which costs $12 per year.

Speedtest.net Speed Test
Free

Whether you're looking for bragging rights that your device has a super speedy Wi-Fi connection or you want proof that your phone's data connection is slower than molasses, Speedtest.net Speed Test gives you the definitive answer. As its name implies, Speedtest.net Speed Test is a simple app that measures the download and upload speeds of your device. You can choose to see the results displayed as kbps, Mbps, or kB/s.

Don't just run the test once and in one spot. Because of the variability of wireless connections, run the test multiple times in different locations so you can see the range of connection speeds your device gets over time.

Where's My Droid
Free

I have an annoying habit of putting my phone down and then promptly forgetting where I left it. If you suffer from the same malady, you need Where's My Droid. By texting or e-mailing a special "attention word" to your phone, you can make your phone play a custom ringtone at full volume — even if the volume had been turned off. You can also text or e-mail a different "attention word for GPS," which sends back a text or e-mail with the phone's coordinates and a link to its location on Google Maps.

Wifi Analyzer
Free (ad supported)

Geek alert: This app requires some networking know-how.

If you live in area where lots of folks have Wi-Fi routers, such as in a large apartment building, you probably have trouble finding a channel for *your* router that isn't already too crowded. The more a particular channel is used by nearby routers, the more those routers interfere with each other, causing slow data transfer speeds. Wifi Analyzer displays all the Wi-Fi routers in the area and shows which channels they're each using, so you can find the least crowded channel to set your router to.

Apple & Macs

iPad For Dummies
978-0-470-58027-1

iPhone For Dummies,
4th Edition
978-0-470-87870-5

MacBook For
Dummies, 3rd Edition
978-0-470-76918-8

Mac OS X Snow
Leopard For
Dummies
978-0-470-43543-4

Business

Bookkeeping For
Dummies
978-0-7645-9848-7

Job Interviews
For Dummies,
3rd Edition
978-0-470-17748-8

Resumes For
Dummies,
5th Edition
978-0-470-08037-5

Starting an
Online Business
For Dummies,
6th Edition
978-0-470-60210-2

Stock Investing
For Dummies,
3rd Edition
978-0-470-40114-9

Successful
Time Management
For Dummies
978-0-470-29034-7

Computer Hardware

BlackBerry
For Dummies,
4th Edition
978-0-470-60700-8

Computers For
Seniors
For Dummies,
2nd Edition
978-0-470-53483-0

PCs For Dummies,
Windows 7 Edition
978-0-470-46542-4

Laptops For
Dummies,
4th Edition
978-0-470-57829-2

Cooking & Entertaining

Cooking Basics
For Dummies,
3rd Edition
978-0-7645-7206-7

Wine For Dummies,
4th Edition
978-0-470-04579-4

Diet & Nutrition

Dieting For Dummies,
2nd Edition
978-0-7645-4149-0

Nutrition For
Dummies,
4th Edition
978-0-471-79868-2

Weight Training
For Dummies,
3rd Edition
978-0-471-76845-6

Digital Photography

Digital SLR Cameras
& Photography For
Dummies, 3rd Edition
978-0-470-46606-3

Photoshop Elements 8
For Dummies
978-0-470-52967-6

Gardening

Gardening Basics
For Dummies
978-0-470-03749-2

Organic Gardening
For Dummies,
2nd Edition
978-0-470-43067-5

Green/Sustainable

Raising Chickens
For Dummies
978-0-470-46544-8

Green Cleaning
For Dummies
978-0-470-39106-8

Health

Diabetes For
Dummies,
3rd Edition
978-0-470-27086-8

Food Allergies
For Dummies
978-0-470-09584-3

Living Gluten-Free
For Dummies,
2nd Edition
978-0-470-58589-4

Hobbies/General

Chess For Dummies,
2nd Edition
978-0-7645-8404-6

Drawing
Cartoons & Comics
For Dummies
978-0-470-42683-8

Knitting For Dummies,
2nd Edition
978-0-470-28747-7

Organizing
For Dummies
978-0-7645-5300-4

Su Doku For
Dummies
978-0-470-01892-7

Home Improvement

Home Maintenance
For Dummies,
2nd Edition
978-0-470-43063-7

Home Theater
For Dummies,
3rd Edition
978-0-470-41189-6

Living the
Country Lifestyle
All-in-One
For Dummies
978-0-470-43061-3

Solar Power Your
Home
For Dummies,
2nd Edition
978-0-470-59678-4

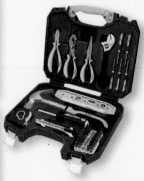